The Mystical Journey to Divine Union

Spiritual Wisdom from Saint John of the Cross

The Mystical Journey to Divine Union

Spiritual Wisdom from Saint John of the Cross

By

John Paul Thomas

My Catholic Life! Inc.

www.mycatholic.life

Copyright © 2018 by My Catholic Life! Inc. All rights reserved. For more on copyright permissions, see mycatholic.life/copyright-permission

Translations of excerpts used from Saint John of the Cross are as follows:

> *Ascent of Mount Carmel*, by Saint John of the Cross, translated by Allison Peers, Third Revised Edition, from the critical edition of P. SILVERIO DE SANTA TERESA, C.D.
>
> *Dark Night of the Soul*, by Saint John of the Cross, translated by David Lewis, 1908.
>
> *Living Flame of Love*, by Saint John of the Cross, translated by David Lewis, First Revised Edition, 1912.
>
> *Spiritual Canticle of the Soul and the Bridegroom Christ*, by Saint John of the Cross, translated by David Lewis, 1908.

Scripture texts in this work are taken from the *New American Bible, revised edition* © 2010, 1991, 1986, 1970 Confraternity of Christian Doctrine, Washington, D.C. and are used by permission of the copyright owner. All Rights Reserved. No part of the New American Bible may be reproduced in any form without permission in writing from the copyright owner.

Cover art: The Holy Trinity, by Antonio de Pereda y Salgado (1611-1678), Museum of Fine Arts, Budapest. Public domain via Wikimedia Commons.

DEDICATION

To our Blessed Mother, the spiritual mother of all Carmelites. May she who was so deeply loved by Saint John of the Cross and Saint Teresa of Ávila, be loved also by each of us with a burning and divine love. May our hearts be set ablaze as we are overshadowed with the Holy Spirit in imitation of the Great Mother of God.

Mother Mary, pray for us. Saint John and Saint Teresa, pray for us. Jesus, I trust in You.

BY

JOHN PAUL THOMAS

"John Paul Thomas" is a pen name chosen by this priest in honor of the Apostles Saints John and Thomas and the great evangelist Saint Paul. This name also evokes the memory of the great Pope Saint John Paul II.

John is the beloved Apostle who sought out a deeply personal and intimate relationship with his Savior. Hopefully the writings in this book point us all to a deeply personal and intimate relationship with our God. May John be a model of this intimacy and love.

Thomas is also a beloved Apostle and close friend of Jesus but is best known for his lack of faith in Jesus' resurrection. Though he ultimately entered into a profound faith crying out, "my Lord and my God," he is given to us as a model of our own weakness of faith. Thomas should inspire us to always return to faith after struggling with doubt. For coming he doubted, doubting he saw, seeing he touched, touching he believed, and believing he shared.

As a Pharisee, Paul severely persecuted the early Christian Church. However, after experiencing a powerful conversion, he went on to become the great evangelist to the gentiles, founding many new communities of believers and writing numerous letters found in Sacred Scripture. His writings are deeply personal and reveal a shepherd's heart. He is a model for all as we seek to embrace our calling to spread the Gospel.

CONTENTS

Introduction	1
Chapter One	19
The Journey Begins	
The Active Night of the Senses	
Chapter Two	47
God Takes the Reigns	
The Passive Night of the Senses	
Chapter Three	73
Growing in Illumination through Contemplation	
The Active Night of the Spirit	
Chapter Four	91
A Third Conversion	
The Passive Night of the Spirit	
Chapter Five	111
The Journey Was Worth It!	
Betrothal and Spiritual Marriage	
Chapter Six	125
Summary and Practical Advice	

INTRODUCTION

Saint John of the Cross is considered by many as the greatest Spiritual Doctor of the Church. This high honor elevates his spiritual writings and adds confidence to those relying upon his wisdom and teaching. He is a true master of the interior life and has left us a treasure of spiritual wisdom in his four main works: *Ascent to Mount Carmel, Dark Night of the Soul, Spiritual Canticle* and *Living Flame of Love*.

These four books combined make up one continuous exposition of mystical theology that peers into the journey each one of us is called to take toward the life of perfect union with God. In his teachings, Saint John especially focuses on two forms of "purgations," or "dark nights," through which every soul must pass in order to achieve perfection in life. What's important to point out is that these purgations, though challenging to embrace, are necessary. They are not optional. For those who do not complete these purgations in this life, Purgatory awaits so as to free the person from everything they are attached to other than God. In the end, holiness is a matter of being attached to and desiring God and God alone.

Mastering Saint John of the Cross and his spiritual teachings could take years or even decades, so go slowly and try to understand one chapter at a time. If a section does not immediately make sense, reread it, ponder it, be open and listen to God. Each chapter will build upon the previous chapter, so it's important to understand what you read before moving on. Let the Holy Spirit be your guide and let the wisdom of Saint John of the Cross lead you into deeper union with our divine Lord.

This book attempts to present the profound theology of Saint John of the Cross in a way that is understandable and accessible to most readers. Because Saint John of the Cross is perhaps the greatest spiritual theologian our Church has ever had, his insights, explanations and wisdom is beyond mere human abilities. Therefore, if you are able to penetrate to the heart of what Saint John has taught, you will be in awe of the depth and breadth of what he has given to the Church.

Biographical Information

Juan de Yepes y Álvarez was born in 1542 (the exact date being unknown) in Fontiveros, Ávila, Spain. His family descended from Jewish converts who settled in Fontiveros. His father, Gonzalo, was an accountant who worked for relatives who were involved in the silk trade. In 1529, Gonzalo married Catalina who was poor and an orphan as a child. This was not well-received by Gonzalo's wealthier family. As a result, he was shunned by his relatives and no longer able to work as their accountant. Therefore, Gonzalo joined his new bride in her trade of weaving to support his own family. Gonzalo and Catalina had three boys: Francisco, Luis and Juan.

In 1545, when John was only three years old, his father died, leaving Catalina to raise and provide for their boys on her own. This was a difficult responsibility for a

Introduction

widow at that time. She sought assistance from Gonzalo's family but was rejected. Therefore, she and her boys lived in destitution. Two years after Gonzalo's death, Luis died of malnutrition. Eventually, Catalina took Francisco and Juan and moved to Medina del Campo, a larger city, and resumed her work as a weaver.

In Medina, Juan was able to attend a boarding school for poor children. He received a basic education, housing and food. Juan proved to be a great student and in 1559 was invited to study at the nearby newly founded Jesuit school when he was 17 years old. With the Jesuits, Juan studied the humanities, grammar, rhetoric, Latin and Greek. Four years later, in 1563, he entered the Carmelite Order taking the name John of St. Matthias.

John made his profession as a Carmelite in 1564 and subsequently received special permission from his superiors to follow the ancient Carmelite rule to the letter rather than embrace the various changes that had taken place in the rule over the years. After his professions, he was sent to study theology and philosophy at the University in Salamanca, which was a very prestigious university. There he excelled in his studies and was known for his intelligence and insights. At the end of his studies, John had second thoughts about his vocation as a Carmelite, preferring instead to live a more contemplative life. As a result, he decided that he would enter the Carthusians once he was ordained. John was indeed ordained a priest in 1567.

Father John returned to Medina to offer his first Mass. However, his intention to join the Carthusians all changed after meeting the Carmelite nun Teresa of Ávila. Mother Teresa was a reformer of the Carmelite

Order and was in Medina to found a new convent. While there, she heard of the newly ordained priest, Father John, and attended his first Mass. Later, she spoke to him about her ideas on reforming the Carmelites in hopes that he would become her first friar in the reform. Father John was intrigued and accepted her invitation to remain a Carmelite and assist her with the new reforms, reviving the ancient rule.

After returning with Mother Teresa to Valladolid, he participated in a period of formation under her guidance and founded the first house for friars along with two other Carmelite brothers. This first house began formally on November 28, 1568. Father John gave up his old name and took on the new name of Father John of the Cross. As more friars joined them, Father John, now the subprior and novice master, moved to a larger house in nearby Alcalá where he also became the rector of the university.

In May of 1572, Mother Teresa asked him to move to Ávila to become the spiritual director for the sisters at the Monastery of the Incarnation. He remained there for five years, working closely with the sisters and growing deep in his own spiritual life. He was especially blessed to act as spiritual director to Mother Teresa who, in many ways, acted as a spiritual guide to him. Shortly after his arrival in 1572, Mother Teresa entered into the spiritual transformation of the divine union while Father John acted as her spiritual director. At times, their conversations led both of them into ecstasy as the Holy Spirit worked powerfully in their lives and through their spiritual friendship.

Sadly, politics had its place in the Church at that time, and there were some who did not like the idea of reforming the Carmelite order. It was in January of 1576 when Father John was arrested for the first time by the more contemporary and well-established Carmelites of the Observance. They wanted to end the reforms of Father John and Mother Teresa and their order that came to be known as the Discalced Carmelites (meaning those who wore sandals rather than shoes). His arrest was quickly ended by the intervention of the papal nuncio, Nicolás Ormaneto, who was favorable toward the reforms of the Discalced Carmelites. However, the following year, in June of 1577, the nuncio died. A new nuncio was appointed who was not in favor of the reforms. Therefore, in December of that year, Father John was once again arrested by the Carmelites of the Observance and put in prison in their monastery in Toledo where he remained for nine months.

Once arrested, the Provincial ordered Father John to "repent" of his reforms and to return to the monastery in Medina. However, Father John refused to do so, arguing that he was not bound by the Provincial's demands, since he had received permission for his work on the reform from the nuncio Ormaneo while he was alive. As a result, Father John was judged as being rebellious and willfully disobedient to their authority and was imprisoned in a small, six-by-ten foot dungeon cell.

During the nine months of his imprisonment, Father John was regularly abused by the friars in attempts to get him to "repent." He was given no change of clothing, very little food, endured a severe case of lice, and was given only his breviary to read. He endured the severe cold of the winter and the heat of the summer in the small dark cell that had only one small window high up on the wall. However, it was during this time of abuse that some of the greatest spiritual treasures to fill our Church were born. Father John, in the darkness of this prison, composed numerous poems, including *The Dark Night of the Soul* and portions of the *The Spiritual Canticle*. God did not allow this abuse to go fruitless. Father John grew deep in the spiritual life and entered into interior freedom through his prayer and surrender to God.

In August of 1578, it is said that God miraculously enabled Father John to escape at night, "in the darkness" as his poem relates, and find refuge with Mother Teresa's sisters in Toledo. Eventually, he escaped to Santa Cruz where he was cared for secretly and nursed back to full health. Over the coming years, his prison experience, the poems he composed, and his life of deep prayer and study prepared him to write four of the greatest works on mystical theology the Church has ever known.

During the year after Father John escaped imprisonment, the Discalced Carmelites did all they could to regularize their situation within the larger Carmelite order and within the Church. Though the new nuncio tried to stop them, the king intervened. In April of 1579, a new provincial was appointed to oversee the Discalced Carmelites and to assist them with their reforms. In 1580, the Holy See allowed the Discalced Carmelites to enjoy independence from the Carmelites of the Observance, and Father John was appointed prior of one of the new monasteries. Mother Teresa died in 1582. In 1585, the Discalced Carmelites were given even greater independence from the Carmelites of the Observance when they were established as an independent province. Father John was elected Vicar Provincial.

Introduction

The charisms of this reform in which Father John and Mother Teresa were so instrumental included the following: 1) a strong Marian devotion, 2) a daily plan carefully set forth to maintain a life of continual prayer, and 3) a strict rule of enclosure focused on the asceticism of solitude, manual labor, perpetual abstinence, fasting, and fraternal charity. Many were attracted to this new strict Carmelite life. Therefore, monasteries of both nuns and friars continued to be founded.

Father John continued to found monasteries and oversee the reform until September of 1591, when he developed gangrene on his leg. He went to a monastery in Ubeda to receive care for his illness. Instead, the superior treated him coldly, arguing that Father John was a burden to the monastery. On December 13, just hours before his death, Father John called the prior to his cell and humbly begged his forgiveness for being a burden. This act of humility completely transformed the prior who was overwhelmed by Father John's sanctity. At midnight, the saintly friar went home to Heaven to his Beloved to sing Matins with the angels, thus completing his mystical journey to divine union.

Outline of Saint John's Teachings

It will be helpful to have a summary outline of the teachings of Saint John of the Cross as presented in his four books. As you read through the various chapters, return to this outline so that you can continually put what you are reading into context. The entire spiritual journey one goes through is presented here in six steps. The first step, "Initial Conversion," is presumed by Saint John but is not covered by him. Therefore, the description is based more on general spiritual theology than on the writings of Saint John. The other five steps are covered in a comprehensive way in his writings.

1. **Initial conversion**—Saint John does not cover this stage, because he presumes the Christian already has purposely entered into it. This is the stage where one turns from a life of sin, embraces Baptism and the effects of Baptism, and begins to walk with God.

2. **Active Night of the Senses**—This process involves the intentional letting go of all worldly attachments to sin. The soul continues to refocus its desires in such a way that everything within its passions and appetites are turned toward God and His holy will.

3. **Passive Night of the Senses**—This is a "purgative contemplation" wherein the person receives a special grace from God that completes the purgation of the sensory appetites begun in the previous step. The soul no longer finds earthly joy and satisfaction in the things of this world and finds its inordinate appetites drying up. This purgation is painful, but the pain helps the soul to focus on God alone. The soul also becomes aware of the presence of the Seven Capital Sins in a new spiritual form. As a result, God even begins to dry up spiritual desires so that the soul will no longer serve God because it "feels good," but rather, because of love alone.

4. **Active Night of the Spirit**—In this stage, the beginner is now a "proficient" in the spiritual life and enjoys an often lengthy period of stability, contemplative prayer and zeal for God. The soul grows in virtue and holiness but begins to sense that God wants more. As a result, the soul begins to allow God to infuse within it the pure gifts of faith, hope and charity. The soul begins to consciously "let go" of its former ideas of God, preferences for its future, and its selfish convictions about God's will. It begins to choose a new level of oneness with God. The intellect begins to have faith in a more general and obscure way, as if it were staring at the Sun. The soul's memory begins to be purified and "forgotten." The will is left in a sort of limbo, waiting upon the moment-by-moment gentle guidance of God.

5. **Passive Night of the Spirit**—This final stage of the final purgation is an action of God in which the spirit enters into what some have termed a "spiritual cocoon." Within the darkness of this cocoon, the intellect, memory and will are completely transformed. The intellect comes to know God in a new way, through darkness and obscurity. The memory is freed from its many images of God and limited imaginations. And the will lets go of everything selfish, becoming attached only to the will of God. There are deep spiritual "piercings" of love experienced in the soul. This love of God not only darkens the soul, it also leaves it humbled, impoverished and empty of all things. But as this happens, the soul is hidden from all enemies—the world, the devil and the flesh. It becomes unhindered and completely

free. As a result, it becomes filled with spiritual strength and fortitude, and clings to God with unshakable fervor. This hidden and secret depth of love and strength, in the most secret core of its spirit, prepares the soul for the glory of divine union.

6. **Divine Union**—The soul has now reached earthly perfection. Every appetite and desire for sin is vanquished. Every desire for the things of this world have been removed. The intellect, memory and will are directed by God in a pure and infused way. The soul now is filled with the sweetest delight of God and, by God, delights in all things as God delights in them. Gratitude floods the soul and every virtue is alive and manifest within the soul. The soul and God are one. The only thing that remains to be gained by the soul is the Beatific Vision of God in Heaven.

Preparation for the Journey

If you were a medical researcher and one day you discovered the cure for cancer, you would not simply say to yourself, "Wow, isn't that interesting. I'll have to hold on to that discovery and perhaps in the future I may want to reveal it to the world." No researcher in his or her right mind would put off the publication of such an incredible discovery. Instead, you would diligently and zealously devote every ounce of energy you had to this amazing discovery, and once it was presented to the world, you would enjoy the countless benefits.

Sadly, when most people discover the "cure" for their life of misery, they fail to embrace that cure with diligence and zeal. The cure is Christ and the pathway to Him is ongoing and deepening conversion. Becoming a Christian is an ongoing process, not only a one-time decision. Once you have come to believe in the Gospel, your journey is just beginning. And the end goal of this journey is not some worldly and passing honor, it's not material wealth, it's not anything the world can offer. The prize is what Saint John of the Cross calls "spiritual marriage" (also called divine union and transforming union). Each one of us is invited by God to embark on this journey toward the perfection of divine union. Hopefully the pages of this book will help to convince you that the discovery of this glorious gift is worth pursuing with your whole heart.

Decide Today

This book is written for those who want to begin the journey to perfection today. Not tomorrow, not next year, not some time in the future. Today. Furthermore, climbing to the summit of perfection is only for those who are willing to do *whatever it takes* in order to achieve their goal. No sacrifice is too great, no detail too small. No hesitation whatsoever can be present.

Perhaps that sounds uninviting, too radical, overwhelming and unreasonable. Well, God is a demanding God, and if you want to enter into divine union here and now, then being 99% committed is not enough. The 1% that is lacking will be like a thin string tied to a bird's leg. No matter how thin the string, unless it is broken, the bird cannot fly away. As Saint John says:

> For it comes to the same thing whether a bird be held by a slender cord or by a stout one; since, even if it be slender, the bird will be well held as though it were stout, for so long as it breaks it not and flies not away. It is true that the slender one is the easier to break; still, easy though it be, the bird will not fly away if it be not broken. And thus the soul that has attachment to anything, however much virtue it possess, will not attain to the liberty of divine union. (*Ascent* XI.4)

So it is with us. If there is the slightest hesitancy, the slightest lack of commitment, the slightest imperfection, we will not enter *fully* into divine union in this life.

Most people will not obtain the perfection of divine union until after death and after the purifying fires of Purgatory. In the end, they will be saints in Heaven. But why choose to wait until death to be purified in Purgatory when you can obtain the infinite blessings of God's inner life while still walking this earth? Why wait? Why hesitate? Why not make the perfection of divine union the one and only goal in life?

You may say, "Well, perfection is one of my goals, but I have other goals also." The problem with that answer is that God will not share you with other goals when it comes to the perfection of divine union. If you want to live perfectly united to God, then God can be your only goal. But don't be confused by that statement. By choosing God and God alone, you are also choosing His perfect will. This means that when you are perfectly immersed in His will and living it as your will, you will find that the joys, satisfactions, fulfillments, relationships, acts of love, beauty, etc. that God wills for you are infinitely greater than any goals for your life that you could come up with on your own.

So why wait? Why hesitate? Why not make the perfection of divine union the exclusive goal of your life? The answer to that question is simple: We are sinners. Sin keeps us lazy, lukewarm, blind, confused, weary, oppressed, etc. In our minds, we often know what we want to do, but we still do not seem to be able to do it. Recall Saint Paul's words:

> What I do, I do not understand. For I do not do what I want, but I do what I hate. Now if I do what I do not want, I concur that the law is good. So now it is no longer I who do it, but sin that dwells in me. For I know that good does not dwell in me, that is, in my flesh. The willing is ready at hand, but doing the good is not. For I do not do the good I want, but I do the evil I do not want. (Romans 7:15-19)

Thus, we face the great paradox of the spiritual life. I do what I don't want to do, and what I want to do I cannot seem to do. Though this is a common experience, when the truth of the Gospel is spoken to our hearts in a deep way, we know it's true. Deep down we all crave the pure truth of Christ. We want Him to convict us, challenge us, change us and make us holy. But all too often that desire remains *deep down* and never rises to the surface.

By presenting a summary overview of Saint John's wisdom and insights in this book, it is hoped that your desire for holiness will well up in you and come to the surface. John's practical insights and unwavering spiritual principles will challenge you and also encourage you. For your part, you need to be open. You need to be serious about growing in holiness. In fact, you need to be serious about growing in perfection! So, if you only want to get just a "little" holier, don't even waste your time. Being "half in" will actually do you more harm than good. The only good attitude is to choose to do whatever it takes to become perfect here and now. No matter what God asks of you, you must be certain that it is worth it. No hesitation, no doubts.

If you are still hesitant, then allow Saint John's insights to challenge you and, hopefully, break you out of your uneasiness. Be open, wide open. Listen carefully, very carefully. Seek the truth, even in the tiniest detail. And be ready and willing to do whatever God leads you to do.

"Beginners" are Not *Beginners*

Saint John of the Cross begins his writings addressing the "beginner." But before presenting the first stage of spiritual development for "beginners," it's important to note that a beginner for Saint John is not what most people may consider a beginner. Saint John does not even deal with the very first stage of spiritual development, which could properly be called "initial conversion."

Initial conversion is what happens when a person encounters Christ in a real and transforming way and decides to turn away from all serious sin in life. Sadly, within the world today, there are many who have not even begun a process of conversion. Many. And they are all around us.

Introduction

Initial conversion may happen at a very young age when a child is slowly introduced to Christ by the faith of his parents, siblings, teachers and others who act as instruments by which faith is imparted. In this case, the child is slowly converted until he or she is old enough to fully choose to follow Christ.

Initial conversion may also happen later in life for those who went astray during their younger years. But no matter the age, a person must encounter the living God, hear His voice calling, and respond generously with faith, turning away from all serious sin.

"This saying is too hard…"

In the Apostle John's Gospel, Chapter 6, Jesus presents His discourse on the most holy Eucharist. People listened, and when Jesus was finished, some said, "This saying is hard; who can accept it?" (John 6:60b) Then we read six verses later, "As a result of this, many [of] his disciples returned to their former way of life and no longer accompanied him" (John 6:66).

The message of the Gospel is challenging. Many will not accept it. Many will get discouraged and walk away. Since Saint John of the Cross presents *not* his own theology but that of the Gospel, we can expect the same reaction. Many will begin to read the lessons of Saint John and say it is too hard, doesn't make sense, is inaccurate, and so on. As a result, many will never finish trying to comprehend this incredible teaching and even fewer will strive to live it in this life, even though they will be bound to finish it in Purgatory.

As you delve into this presentation of the teaching of Saint John, it's important to expect to be greatly challenged by what is taught. Do not expect to be able to accomplish total transformation in Christ quickly and easily. Saint John tells us that very few people in this life actually attain divine union. In fact, few people even make it through the first step that is covered in the first chapter. Keep reminding yourself it is worth it and persevere.

Additionally, it should be noted that the teachings of Saint John are written as an <u>explanation</u> of what happens in the spiritual life and what you will experience along the way of your spiritual journey to perfection. Understanding the process will assist in walking that path. Be open and use the wisdom of Saint John as your guide.

Where am I at?

One last thing to mention before we enter into the teaching of Saint John, is that many will find themselves pondering the question, "Where am I at?" Meaning, as you read through the various levels of spiritual development, you may find yourself constantly trying to figure out which stage you are currently at. Don't do that. The better approach to reading this book is to simply read it and try to understand the overview of the entire process of spiritual development. Then, when it is understood, God will bring various lessons you have learned to mind at the right time. Therefore, pay attention to anything that jumps out at you and especially anything that strikes a nerve. When that happens, be it today or some time in the future, pay attention to that lesson.

Introduction

This entire process is not always completely linear. In other words, you may find that some lessons from various chapters assist you here and now, while others will assist you later on. Thus, if the teachings on attachments and worldly desires speak to you, pay attention to those. If you find that the teachings on meditation are fruitful in your life, then work on meditation. If you can relate to the signs of the various levels of contemplation, then work on practicing that. And if you are experiencing the signs of darkness, aridity, dryness or spiritual annihilation, then that section is for you. Pay attention to that which speaks to you and you will certainly be helped along the way on your road to perfection!

Chapter One

The Journey Begins

The Active Night of the Senses

If you are ready to make the radical choice to do whatever it takes to obtain the high calling to total transformation in Christ (divine union), then take note that the first step will be painful. But the "pain" will be purifying and ultimately will end in sweetness, interior stillness, freedom, peace and repose.

As mentioned in the Introduction, a "beginner" for Saint John of the Cross is one who is *all in,* so to speak, and has already established a life of prayer, but has not yet surrendered fully to the will of God. If that is you, then it is time to let God draw you deeper into a life of prayer so as to enter through what Saint John calls the "night of the senses."

The night of the senses is one of two "dark nights" through which every soul must pass in order to achieve divine union (also called spiritual marriage and transforming union). This first dark night, the night of the senses, is divided into two parts: *active* and *passive*. This chapter will attempt to present Saint John's teaching for beginners on the *active night of the senses*.

Summary of the "Active Night of the Senses"

The goal of the "active night of the senses" is to free your soul from the lowest forms of pleasure, so that you can more fully seek God who also produces within you the highest form of spiritual delight, resulting from the perfection of divine union with Him. This first step is just that: the first step. Once a person walks through this initial purgation of their appetites and desires, God will take them through three more levels of purgation. But the first step is where we begin.

In this step, the person must engage in intentional acts of self-denial and must also seek to know God in a new and deeper way through the prayer of meditation. Selfishness must be stripped away, and all the deceptive pleasures flowing from sinful attachments and unhealthy desires must be eliminated.

The reason for this is that we are easily deceived about that which is good for us. In the beginning of our spiritual journey, we still cling to the pleasure that comes from sin and from the many other things of this world. We may still believe that the things that satisfy us are money, sensual delights, excessive food or the satisfaction of other disordered cravings. And while those things do produce a certain form of temporary delight, the end result is slavery and bondage. Therefore, God wants you free. So this first step involves <u>you</u> making specific choices to turn away from these deceptive attachments and desires while, at the same time, you grow in your knowledge of the glorious truths that God wants to reveal to you.

Prayer Proper to the "Beginners"

It's important to note the form of prayer proper to each stage of spiritual development. In this first stage, the person must regularly practice the prayer of meditation. Meditation simply means you engage your mind in the Scripture or some other inspiring truth of God. When God is calling you to this beginning stage of prayer, you will regularly be "inspired" by grace and, at times, take great delight in the things of God. Your soul will feel God's closeness and will find great joy in spiritual things, such as long periods of prayer, fastings, spiritual reading and works of charity.

This life of meditation, inspiration and consolation is the way that God initially nourishes the soul as if it were a small infant. The infant is fed pure warm milk, caressed, carried, and treated with delicate care. All of these delicacies and consolations are from God and assist the soul during the active night of the senses. Later, during the *passive* night of the senses, God begins to change the person's prayer and their relationship with Him to that of a spiritual child or adolescent rather than an infant. This child will then grow further, becoming more spiritually mature, reaching adulthood through a deeper form of prayer called contemplation. Eventually, the person will reach a state of perfection (divine union) and will live a life fully united to God through habitually sustained contemplation.

Let's now look at some of the philosophical language Saint John of the Cross uses for his teachings on the active night of the senses. This language may be new to some, but it is important to understand, so study it attentively.

Defining the Language

So, what is the "active night of the senses?" Simply put, this refers to the initial actions that <u>you</u> must do in order to grow in holiness once you have begun your spiritual journey. Some things you can only accomplish by a special grace of God (Chapter Two and Four will focus on these). But initially, there are many things you <u>actively</u> must do in order to move forward in your spiritual journey.

The key concept you must begin with is "purgation" or "dark night." Though Saint John will speak of varying levels of purgation, this term will mainly be used in this chapter to describe the *voluntary purgations* that you must go through, so as to obtain *freedom* from all of your *attachments* to inordinate *pleasures* you have formed by giving in to your *sensory appetites and desires*. Let's carefully define each one of these italicized words so that you are prepared to understand the beautiful wisdom given to us by Saint John in regard to this first active purgation.

Sensory: This refers to everything you come to know and experience through your five senses. To understand what a "sensory" experience is, imagine that you had lost all five senses. What would you experience in this world? Nothing! You'd be pure spirit. You could still think, remember and make acts of your will, but you would not be able to receive anything into your sensory appetites from this world. Imagine further if you had never had access to any of your five senses. In that case, you would not even have any memories or concepts that come from this world via your senses. You would still think and will, but only on a purely spiritual level like the angels. Thus, everything you see, touch, smell, feel or hear in this physical world feeds your sensory appetites. Everything you do purely in your mind and will make up your spiritual sensory appetites when that thinking and willing is based on that which initially came to you through your five senses.

Appetites: Human beings were created with appetites. There is no escaping this experience, since it is a natural part of who we are. God made us with the natural ability to be drawn to what we perceive as good. For example, if you were working all day in the hot sun and you began to become dehydrated, your body would naturally crave water. You cannot not desire this. It's how you were made. The key to understanding your appetites is to realize that you always desire that which your appetites perceive as good. It's impossible to desire something that you perceive as bad. Even if the desire you have is, in fact, bad for you, you will not desire it *because* you perceive it as bad; rather, you will desire it because your appetites are confused and perceive the object of your desire as something good.

Another important distinction to make regarding the various appetites we have is that there are natural appetites and voluntary ones. A natural appetite comes from natural inclinations within your senses, such as in the above example of desiring water when thirsty. These appetites have little or no moral significance in and of themselves unless they become indulgent. The voluntary appetites, however, are the ones that are more concerning. These are desires we have that originated because of some decision we made, such as choosing a sin, or choosing to give in to a natural appetite in an indulgent way.

To illustrate a voluntary appetite, let's consider an extreme example. Let's say someone is addicted to a very powerful drug such as heroin. The truth is that another dose of heroine is not good for that person. But nonetheless, the person who is addicted to heroin desires the drug because the appetites are enslaved to this drug and the appetites are drawn to the satisfaction that comes from the euphoric feeling of pleasure the body receives when taking the drug. Therefore, intellectually the person knows that the drug is not good, but the appetites desire it anyway because the appetites are misled and perceive this drug as good. And this appetite <u>originated</u> in the initial willed or *voluntary* choice to use heroin. Of course, the addictive nature of this drug makes it even worse, but the key concept to understand here is that you don't have a *natural* desire for heroin when you are conceived. It only comes after you willingly tried it out. Thus, it is a *voluntary appetite*. More will be said on this shortly in the section entitled "voluntary."

Attachments: An attachment is what results from habitually choosing that which you desire. To illustrate, consider again the heroin addict. He is <u>attached</u> to heroin because he has given in to the desire for it time and time again. He has allowed his bodily appetites to take delight in the drug and, as a result, he is attached to it. He is addicted. Though a heroin addiction is an extreme example, the same principle applies to everything you become attached to. For example, you become attached to money when you choose, over and over, to give in to the appetite for money. This attachment applies even if you have very little money. The appetite for more leaves you attached and desiring more. The problem is not that you do or do not have money; rather, the problem is being attached to the desire for it. Other examples include the appetite for a certain kind of food, entertainment, satisfaction, pleasure, and so on. These become *attachments* when you allow your appetites for these things to form habits within you. Though you may start with a *natural* appetite for something (such as a particular food), you become attached to it when you voluntarily choose it in an indulgent way. You can also become attached to immaterial things, such as the praise and honor others give you or fail to give you. When you desire the praise of others, and then continually act in such a way so as to receive that praise, you become attached to the praise.

Similarly, a dog also has appetites and attachments. For example, a dog may learn tricks and perform them, because it forms a habit of desiring the praise of its owner. This attachment to praise (or a tasty treat) is what enables a dog to do one trick after another at the command of the owner. A dog is controlled by its appetite and the memory of the reward. The praise (or the treat) causes a delight and, as a result, it is sought over and over. One difference between us and animals is that an animal cannot freely choose to be purified of its appetites. We can. An animal is purely sensory, affectionate and ruled by appetites. We have a free will that can override our sensory appetites.

Voluntary: A voluntary action is one that you freely make. Specifically, for the purpose of understanding the lessons in this chapter, a voluntary action is one that you make *prior* to forming a habit. This is an important distinction because once a habit is formed, your actions are less voluntary. Again, a heroin addict often experiences a loss of freedom and, therefore, no longer makes completely voluntary decisions each time he takes the drug on account of the addiction. An attachment weakens your ability to freely choose in a voluntary way. You act out of habit rather than freedom, just like animals. This applies to every habit you form. If you habitually use foul language, speak gossip, desire money, or form any other habit, you become less and less free to make voluntary actions. However, as a human being with a free will and intellect, you can always work to undo the habitual attachments you have voluntarily formed.

A true voluntary action is one you make with the full consent of your will. If the choice you freely make is for a grave sin, then you become a slave to that sin and attached to it. If the completely free choice you make is for a venial sin or some lesser spiritual imperfection, then you become attached to that sin or imperfection. And if the completely free choice you make is to habitually indulge in some natural appetite you have (such as for chocolate), then you will form an attachment to that natural desire. However, if the completely free choice you make is for some virtue, flowing from God Himself, then you also grow in the virtuous habit and become attached to God more completely.

Pleasure: The word "pleasure" does not need much of an explanation. But for our purposes, there is a twofold distinction that must be made. One form of pleasure comes from unhealthy (or inordinate) desires, and the other flows from union with God. Unhealthy pleasures enslave, distract and confuse you. But the good form of pleasure increases and changes according to the extent that your soul is united to God in divine union. In this case, even friendships and other natural goods are more purely enjoyed when your soul is united to God. In other words, the holier you become, the more capable you are of taking <u>true</u> delight in all that God sets before you.

Purgation: Purgation sounds like a painful word, and indeed it is. But purgation is more than just painful, it's also freeing. Purgation is the process one must go through to remove bad habits and attachments to anything and everything other than God and His perfect will. This purgation is a process of complete interior *detachment* from everything that is not God. Purgation is at the heart of Saint John's teaching and will be the central focus of any soul seeking the perfection of divine union. As mentioned earlier, purgation in the spiritual life takes on two forms: active and passive. "Active" means those actions that <u>you can do</u> to be freed of your unhealthy attachments. "Passive" means not resisting those things that <u>God does in you</u> to help finish the purgation you have started. Your responsibility in passive purgation is simply to consent to the work God is doing within you. Passive purgation is necessary for perfection, because you cannot fully free yourself by your own effort. Only God can ultimately accomplish complete freedom from every unhealthy attachment within your soul.

Freedom: Freedom is what happens in your soul when you complete your purgation. It is experienced in two ways. First, when an attachment is purified from your soul, you are set free from that which bound you and are no longer weighed down and oppressed by your sinful habits. Second, once you are set free from your unhealthy attachments, you are more capable of freely choosing God and His perfect will in your life. This liberation produces great joy! You are then able to truly exercise your free will in a new and complete way. And when you use this free will to choose God and His perfect will, there is no end to the experience of liberty you will enjoy.

Pleasure as Your Goal

Before we get into the dark night and the many purgations your soul must go through in order to achieve transforming union with God, it might be helpful to "ease the pain," so to speak, by offering a hopeful and encouraging reason to fully embrace every purgation of your soul. The reason is that purgation is the only way to obtain the greatest satisfaction, fulfillment and, yes, pleasure in life.

God wants you happy. Happier than you could ever imagine! He wants you fulfilled. To a greater degree than you desire for yourself! He even wants you to take great delight in every aspect of your daily life. He wants every meal you eat, every hobby in which you partake, every relationship with which you are blessed and every action of your day to be sources of unfathomable pleasure and sweet delight. But in order for that to happen, there must first be a purgation of your entire self so that you engage your daily life in a new way. Furthermore, there has to be a discovery of the essential spiritual truth that the passing pleasures of this world are like dust in comparison to the delights that God wants to bestow upon you. Therefore, any purgation of a lower form of "pleasure" will ultimately result in the enjoyment of so much more.

Sometimes people can misconstrue Saint John of the Cross as a saint of pain and sorrow. The concept of entering into purgation and the dark night can be

The Journey Begins

frightening and uninviting when misunderstood. But when understood properly, Saint John reveals to us that more joy, delight and purified pleasure awaits us than we could ever obtain on our own. And the delight is of a much higher level than we are even aware that exists.

Think about the worldly image of the hedonistic "pleasure seeker." This is the person who lives for the moment, lives the high life, is always seeking greater adventures or new experiences that the world can offer. Well, the truth is that when a person makes it their goal to seek every pleasure the world can offer, they may end up obtaining just that! And that is a sad result! Why? Because the pleasures of the world, even if one were to be able to indulge in all of them, are like pure torture and filth compared to the incomprehensible joys of a life lived in the transformation of divine union. There is simply no comparison.

So, does God want you to enjoy life and take pleasure in it? Most certainly. But He wants your pleasure to be of the <u>highest order</u>, the order for which you were made, the eternal delights, the spiritual delights. He does not want you to selfishly indulge in passing and finite pleasures that never fully satisfy and always leave you hungry for more. God wants you satisfied, not hungry. He wants you at rest, not always anxious. He wants your heart to be overflowing with joy, not always craving for more.

Here are a few lines taken from Book I, Ch. IV, #4-5 of the *Ascent of Mount Carmel* that illustrate the comparison between seeking fulfillment in the world vs. seeking fulfillment in God:

> ...all the grace and beauty of the creatures, compared with the grace of God, is the height of misery and of uncomeliness.
>
> ...all the goodness of the creatures of the world, in comparison with the infinite goodness of God, may be described as wickedness.
>
> All the wisdom of the world and all human ability, compared with the infinite wisdom of God, are pure and supreme ignorance...

In other words, if a person were to obtain everything the world holds up as beautiful, good and wise, what they actually obtain is misery, wickedness and ignorance when compared to that which God wants to give them through divine union. If that is difficult to understand and accept, don't get discouraged just yet. For now, simply accept the fact that the fulfillment, joy, pleasure and delight that God wants to bestow upon you through divine union is infinitely more fulfilling, joyful, pleasurable and delightful than what the world can give or than you can obtain on your own by satiating all of your appetites. Even if you were to obtain the greatest material wealth, enjoy the best entertainment, daily eat the finest food, be greatly esteemed by the world, learn every bit of knowledge humanly possible, etc., you would still be absolutely miserable in comparison to what God wants to give you. Keep this in the forefront of your mind as you now look at the beginning process of purgation.

The Truth Leads to Purgation

If "purgation" sounds painful, difficult and depressing, that is because you have allowed yourself to be deceived by the world, the flesh, the evil one and your own misguided will. Do you want the *truth*, or do you prefer to live in a *lie*? That's actually a difficult question to answer for many people. Many people choose to remain in a state of ignorance rather than face the glorious truth God wants to speak to them. Why? Because if they remain in ignorance, they do not have to change. They can go on pretending they are happy and can continue seeking pleasure in all the easy worldly and fleshly appetites they have. Purgation begins when the lies are revealed and unmasked. You must first come to know the Truth so that the Truth can set you free.

Identifying Your Attachments and Desires

It's now time to begin getting practical by looking at what happens within your soul in regard to attachments and desires on a sensory level. Here are some concrete examples of "sensory attachments and desires" offered in no particular order:

- Being very talkative
- Desiring wealth
- Desiring food prepared in a particular way
- Desiring excessive amounts of food or drink
- Wanting the most comfortable amenities
- Desiring a promotion at work
- Wanting to go first
- Desiring disordered sexual gratification

- Desiring the finest clothes and other belongings
- Clinging to a person in a selfish way
- Wanting others to notice you
- Being overly curious about the latest gossip
- Regularly being attached to your mobile phone, tablet or social media
- Desiring always the easiest way
- Desiring the best of things
- Having an extreme love of your possessions
- Etc., etc., etc.

Now it may be the case that as you read that short list of examples, you find yourself guilty of every one of them. Ouch, the truth may actually hurt. It may be painful to go through the slow and careful process of discovering why these and so many other attachments you have in life actually do you far more harm than you realize. If you are attached to the things above or to any other similar thing, you will probably be tempted to immediately justify your attachment and come up with all sorts of reasons as to why they are good, or at least OK. Do not fear. The process of purgation may be slow and painful but remember that it is also renewing and freeing. It's the only way to true joy and pleasure.

It's important to note that some items in the above list are far worse for the soul than others. And the list is not referring to natural preferences, likes or dislikes. For example, if you like spicy food or the color blue, there is no way to unlike spicy food or the color blue. But that's not the goal. There is nothing wrong with liking one thing or another. But Saint John does clearly teach that if you want to obtain the heights of perfection, all of your natural likes and dislikes must be tempered and brought into order by God's divine grace, so they do not become indulgent, resulting in inordinate attachments. In other words, your natural preferences cannot control you, they cannot have an unhealthy hold on you. In fact, the only way to *truly* enjoy the natural likes and dislikes you have is to make sure that they are tempered by God's grace and that the desire for them is properly ordered within your appetites.

The list above could go on for pages. In Chapter Six of this book, there is a thorough examination of conscience that will help you to identify many of your attachments and unhealthy desires. For now, the goal is to get a basic understanding of attachments and desires and to begin accepting the fact that you have attachments and desires that need to be purified, if you are going to be fully happy in life by entering into divine union.

Do I have to Give up EVERY Attachment?

I'm happy to tell you that the answer to that question is absolutely "Yes!" Yes, you do have to be purified of EVERY single *attachment*, no matter how small, if you want to *fully* enter into the unfathomable joys and fulfillment of divine union. Not a single disordered attachment can remain (note that all *attachments* to things other than God are disordered). Certainly nothing that is seriously sinful (mortal), nor anything that is only somewhat sinful (venial). But Saint John goes even further. He says that we not only have to overcome our mortal and venial sins, we also have to overcome every spiritual imperfection, no matter how small, if we want to enter into divine union. And in the coming chapters, he will take us even further than that!

Why is it that every single attachment must go? Because divine union means the soul is one with God in every way. It means God has taken complete possession of you. Recall the words of Saint Paul: "(Y)et I live, no longer I,, but Christ lives in me" (Galatians 2:20). A soul that is completely conformed to Christ is also detached from every sin and imperfection, because conformity to Christ and attachment to sin are not compatible. Even those who live in a state of perfect divine union will still "fall seven times a day" (Proverbs 24:16), meaning that they will still commit a venial sin here or there, but they will do so without those momentary sins becoming <u>habits</u>, or attachments to sin or imperfection.

Attachments AND Desires

Another important insight that Saint John of the Cross offers us is that the purgation of our attachments is not enough. We must also be purified of all <u>voluntary</u> desires for anything other than God and His will. Remember that a *voluntary* desire is different than a *natural* one. Voluntary desires create attachments. An attachment means that we have formed a habit that is either sinful or simply imperfect. For example, if you have a habit of entering into gossip, this means that you have chosen to engage in gossip over and over. You are bound to a certain extent to that tendency and experience a certain lack of freedom in choosing this sin. Breaking free of this habit is the same as detaching from that sin. But detachment is not enough. The *voluntary* desire to gossip must also be purified. This means that if an occasion arises in which you are invited to engage in gossip, but you have already overcome the perpetual habit of doing so, you are free to choose to enter back into gossip or not. If, when presented with the opportunity to gossip, you are tempted but immediately dismiss the temptation, then you are also becoming more and more free of the voluntary desire and will immediately grow stronger in virtue every time you immediately dismiss the temptation. And when the opposite virtue grows strong, you will eventually find gossip repulsive, and future temptations will be more easily dismissed. If, however, you voluntarily *consider* engaging in the gossip, and take even one step toward doing so, even if you stop, you are still slightly bound by the voluntary desire and it will remain, and perhaps even grow stronger. Though this is not nearly as serious as habitually consenting to a sin, it still must be purified. Therefore, true freedom involves the immediate and complete habitual renunciation of even the voluntary desire for sin or the desire for a voluntary attachment to anything that is not God. Though *temptation* is not a sin or imperfection (recall that even Jesus was tempted), voluntarily entertaining and considering the temptation keeps you from the perfection of divine union until the habitual desire is eliminated. It's like that small, thin string tied to the leg of a bird. It may not be that hard to break the string, but until that string is broken, the bird cannot fly free.

Perhaps this sounds like an extreme expectation. Well, it is extreme. But remember that we are describing here that which is necessary to obtain perfection! Perfection means just that: perfection. And though few will obtain it in this life, it is possible, and it is ultimately necessary if we are to enter fully into the Beatific Vision of Heaven.

Furthermore, it must be made clear that there is no way to eliminate natural desires or even sinful temptations. And that is not even the goal we should have. For example, if you like blueberries then it is not necessary that you try to dislike them. We all have natural likes and dislikes. The goal is not to become completely indifferent to everything in life. That would be a denial of natural goods. Rather, the goal is to keep all of your natural likes and dislikes in check, in a balanced and temperate way. So, if you like to go fishing, or like to sew, or like to eat steak, that's fine. Enjoy them at times and let them be a source of refreshment. But make sure that these likes and dislikes do not take possession of you and do not so consume you that you begin to engage in them in an indulgent manner. When this happens, you will find your desires torn between those attachments and God. And when your desires are divided, they cannot be fully centered on God and His holy will.

And in regard to temptations, you cannot eliminate them. The devil, the flesh and the world will continually tempt you in numerous ways. God permits these temptations so that you can make the right choice and, thus, grow in virtue. You must learn to habitually turn away from temptations, thus eliminating even the desire for them. When this happens, temptations will be like a rubber ball bouncing off an iron wall. The ball still hits the wall, but the ball has no effect.

A Proper Ordering of Your Voluntary Desires

It may be helpful to clarify further this radical teaching about the purgation of one's <u>voluntary</u> desires by considering a practical example of how a well-ordered soul will deal with its natural inclinations, likes and dislikes, and

The Journey Begins

not allow them to turn into habitual, excessive and unhealthy attachments.

Let's say that you are blessed with a lovely home and enjoy its contents very much. However, by God's grace you are not overly attached to it even though you enjoy it. You have many nice things, but God helps you keep your interior attachment to your home under control. What would happen if some unfortunate situation occurred, such as a house fire, and many of your belongings were lost?

Most likely, your initial reaction would understandably be disappointment. That's just a natural reaction. However, if your interior desires are well ordered by God, then you would quickly remind yourself that it's not the end of the world. In fact, it's no big deal. You would begin to realize that you have been given the wonderful opportunity to manifestly practice your faith by embracing the virtues of poverty of spirit and interior detachment. Thus, rather than becoming angry and depressed, you would see the spiritual blessings God brings from this experience, and you would rejoice even though there is a very real temptation to be upset.

This level of interior detachment is difficult to achieve, but it is necessary if you are going to obtain divine union. God calls some people to literally give up everything and follow Him as a religious monk or nun. But to everyone else, He requires that they live within the world with a spirit of interior detachment and poverty of spirit toward all things. The things of this world are not bad, in and of themselves, and many of the things of the world can give enjoyment. But it is only true enjoyment when we remain interiorly detached from everything, seeing all we have as a gift, not as a self-satisfying possession.

The same could be applied to any natural desire, like or dislike. In the end, as long as that which you like is not sinful, and as long as you could easily give it up if you had to or if it were taken away, then you are in a great position to actually enjoy those simple delights of life. The food you eat will become even more delicious, the hobbies you engage in will become even more enjoyable and refreshing, and the relationships you have will be even more fruitful. And those delights will then become a habitual source of gratitude, and they will foster your deeper love of God and of all good things in and through God.

Another way to illustrate this spiritual principle is to consider your relationship with another person. Perhaps it is your spouse, a child, parent or friend. Friendships have the potential of being sources of great joy when they are entered into with freedom and detachment. But when they are experienced as clingy, needy, obsessive or possessive, they are a burden—and not a true friendship. Interestingly, the only way to give and receive love between persons is to be detached from that person in your selfish appetites and affections. Perhaps that sounds strange, but it's true. Even spouses must live in selfless detachment to each other if they wish to give and receive love freely. When someone clings to you and demands your attention and affection, they are not able to truly love you or be loved by you. All they can experience is the fleeting satisfaction of their demands for affection being fulfilled. But that's not love, that's a disordered affection. When you are detached from another and they are detached from you, and subsequently they freely offer their love to you and you freely offer your love to them,

The Journey Begins

then the joy experienced by that freely given friendship is far more than any selfish affection can achieve.

To illustrate how we are to love in a detached way, consider this true story of two loving parents. One day, their daughter became quite ill. She was taken to the doctor's office for an exam and while there she fainted. The doctor could not revive her and an ambulance was immediately called. The parents watched as paramedics frantically worked on resuscitating their daughter, and they sensed the seriousness of this situation. The parents were aware that their daughter may not survive.

As their daughter was placed in the ambulance, the loving parents followed behind to the emergency room. However, while following the ambulance, instead of giving in to despair, anger or fear, they immediately began praying in the following way:

> "Dear Lord, we thank You for the life of our daughter Ann. You gave her to our care and now in this moment we surrender her to You alone. If it be Your will that she survives this illness, so be it. If it be Your will that Ann is taken from us and from this world, then so be it. Dear Lord, Ann is Your daughter and we entrust her to Your perfect love. Amen."

Such a prayer would be difficult for many parents to pray. Instead, many would understandably be filled with fear and be crying out a prayer more like this:

> "Please, God, heal her! Don't take her from us! Please, we beg You! We love our daughter and

> hope for a long life with her. Please, Jesus, heal her! We need You!"

Try to carefully consider the difference between these two prayers. The second form of prayer is quite understandable and flows from a certain level of love. However, this love is more based on fear and a sense of ownership, and actually hinders the purest form of love for their daughter. The focus is more upon the parents' fear of losing their daughter and all the hopes they have for her. Again, this prayer is very understandable given the circumstances. However, the first prayer is far more perfect because of the detachment from all selfishness in the parents' relationship with their daughter. There is also a profound trust in God's love for her. In the first prayer, the trust and total surrender of their daughter to God is what opens the door for these parents to manifest a genuinely pure love for their daughter. They do not love her because they "need" her and fear losing her. Rather, their loving *detachment* from her actually has the effect of them being able to love her in freedom and to be more fully united to her in accord with the perfect will of God.

As you ponder the detachment and purgation of your desires, be it to persons, food, clothing, material items, or something that is immaterial (such as the admiration of another), keep in the forefront of your mind that total detachment is the only way to enjoy those persons or things from which you detach. That's one reason why total detachment is so good. Not only does it free you to love God with your whole heart, mind, soul and strength, it also enables you to love others and be loved by others and to experience the joys of these loves.

The Primary Reason for Purgation

Though there are numerous blessings of pleasure and joy you can receive when you are detached, the primary reason to seek total detachment from all inordinate affections and desires is to dispose yourself for union with God, the ultimate source of fulfillment in life. The effects of union with God are numerous and, in fact, infinite. Union with God makes everything in life better. But the primary reason for union with God is not just to make everything in life better. It's first and foremost for the simple reason of *being in union with God!* Love of God is what we are made for and He must become the single center of our lives. Only when this happens will every other aspect of our lives be ordered toward the single goal of divine union. Furthermore, when this happens, God and God alone becomes the source of our delight and fulfillment. Delighting in God with every fiber of your being is infinitely superior to sharing your desires with other lesser or disordered satisfactions.

For example, it is not a contradiction to say that you must love God with *all* your heart, *all* your mind, *all* your soul and with *all* your strength and to then say you also love your spouse, family, certain hobbies, etc. This is a great mystery in that the only way to true love of others is to give yourself 100% to God. All means all. Think about that. Normal human logic may lead you to think that you should love God with most of your heart, but that there are many other things to love in life. Therefore, as long as you love God more than other things, you are doing well. Right? Wrong. God wants all of you, completely, without reserve. He is to be the exclusive focus of <u>your</u> *human love*. But the good news is that, because God is Omnipotent, He is able to then take the human love you offer Him and transform it into the superabundance of His *divine love*, so that He overflows in your life and He loves others in and through you. God does the loving; you are the instrument. But the blessing, when God is the exclusive focus of your human love, is that you are able to share in the divine blessings of love that are offered to others, through you, by God, in exchange for the human love you offer God. Thus, the love you have for your spouse, since it overflows from the divine love of God in your heart to your spouse, is in fact divine love. And the joy that comes from that love, offered by God through your human heart, is in fact divine joy. Why settle for merely human joys when you can experience divine joys every day?

Does Purgation Hurt?

Yes, but sin hurts worse. The purgation of your senses, either in an active or passive way, will be painful. Severing the chains, cords or even the tiny strings that bind you to your appetites, attachments and desires will produce pain in your sensory appetites.

So as to prepare you for the experience of being purified, Saint John of the Cross spends much time talking about the experience of purgation being like a dark night. He explains that as a person is fully purified of each disordered attachment and desire, there will be a feeling of loss, emptiness, nakedness and nothingness. Their soul is now "all stilled." But in that stillness, until the soul replaces its former attachments with God, the feeling of interior loss can be quite painful. Initially, the passions and appetites will feel as if they are lost and empty. They will miss their former attachments and will be restless. Recall Saint Augustine's famous line, "Our hearts are restless, O Lord, until they rest in You." In other words, when attachments and desires are severed, there is a restlessness that can only be calmed and satiated by God Himself. This restlessness leaves the soul in a sort of darkness.

But that's OK, and, in fact, it's good! The key is to identify the darkness that is felt as the first step toward freedom. The soul must remain still and at peace in this state until God enters in and takes the place of all former delights. So if you are "addicted" to chocolate in an excessive way and you work to break that inordinate attachment, you can expect to feel the loss of that satisfaction on a sensory level. It hurts not to be able to satiate your craving for chocolate. But as time goes on, the soul that breaks attachments to things of this world out of love for God will have their former "cravings" satiated by their love of God alone. And they may eventually even be able to enjoy the pleasure of chocolate in a purified and elevated way, once their unhealthy attachment is broken.

If you are uneasy with the idea of experiencing painful purgations, then consider the following as a good motivation. Regarding pain, Saint John explains that disordered attachments and imperfections actually cause far more interior suffering than the purgation of the senses causes. So, while it is true that going through a purgation is painful, what is far more painful is to perpetually remain unpurified, attached to sin, and attached to our disordered desires.

First, disordered attachments deprive us of the fullness or the Spirit of God, that is, they deprive us of full union with God. And that absence in our lives is painful. We may think that the agony we experience here or there is the fault of our circumstances or perhaps what someone else did to us, but it's not true. Most of our interior suffering is caused by not being in full union with God. By analogy, would a fish suffer if it jumped out of water for a while? Indeed! A fish is made for water and when removed it will suffer and ultimately die. So it is with us. We are made for God. And when we lack perfect union with Him, we feel the effects. We suffer. And if we do not eventually enter into union with Him, we will also die.

Secondly, the sins and disordered desires themselves bring sufferings and afflictions to the soul. Saint John offers five forms of suffering that afflict us on account of attachment to sin. He says that these disordered desires cause the soul to be *weary*, *tormented*, *darkened*, *defiled* and *weakened*. So, while it is true that going through a purgation is painful, what is far more painful is to perpetually remain unpurified, attached to sin, and attached to our disordered desires. Let's look at each of these briefly:

Weary: Attachments and desires do not refresh the soul, even when they are satiated. In fact, the opposite happens. When an appetite is fed, or a desire given in to, the soul becomes tired, weakened and wearied.

Tormented: Attachments inflict turmoil and interior suffering on a soul. When an attachment is strong, the torment is stronger. The more the appetite is fed, the more the restlessness.

Darkened: Attachments confuse a soul and cloud its intellect. It is no longer able to see the Truth of God clearly. The soul's experience is like looking for the sun on a very foggy day.

Defiled: Attachments rob the soul of its beauty. The soul begins feeling filthy and dirty, like a beautiful gold chalice being covered in tar.

Weakened: The greater the attachment, the weaker the soul becomes. And the weaker the soul becomes, the more it gives in to sin and, thus, becomes even weaker in its fight against sin.

"Kindled in Love with Yearnings…"

Hopefully, the spiritual insights of this chapter have helped you to understand the importance of trying to actively purify and free yourself of every inordinate attachment and desire. If you felt quite challenged, hopefully you can humbly and honestly look at your attachments and make a plan to begin letting go of them. Here is a summary of what you must seek to be detached from:

1. The commission of every mortal sin
2. Habitual venial sins
3. Habitual spiritual imperfections
4. Every voluntary habitual desire that leads you to form an attachment within your appetites to anything other than God

Be assured that you cannot do this on your own. But you must begin the arduous process. If you do not begin, God cannot complete it in you. And if God does not complete this purgation in you, then Purgatory will be required of you after death. But as has been mentioned, it is irrational to wait until Purgatory. There are too many wonderful reasons to seek this purgation now. In fact, Saint John says very clearly that those who are purified in Purgatory do not grow in merit and glory, only purgation. But those who grow in perfection here and now also gain much merit in Heaven and obtain a much greater eternal glory.

At the end of Book I of the *Ascent of Mount Carmel*, the book in which Saint John of the Cross presents his theology on the active night of the senses, he explains that the only way to become fully purified of every sensory attachment is by a special grace from God. This grace will "kindle" the soul with "yearnings" for God. These desires for God will become so strong that they will ultimately eliminate every single attachment the soul has formed.

Chapter Two

God Takes the Reigns

The Passive Night of the Senses

> You were dead in your transgressions and sins in which you once lived following the age of this world, following the ruler of the power of the air, the spirit that is now at work in the disobedient. All of us once lived among them in the desires of our flesh, following the wishes of the flesh and the impulses, and we were by nature children of wrath, like the rest. (Ephesians 2:1-3)

This Scripture reveals three enemies of our souls: the world, the flesh and the devil. What if you could be completely free from the influences of all three of these evils? What if the world and its many enticements were of no interest to you. Or if the many disordered desires of your fleshly appetites were eliminated? Or if the devil himself were to have no influence over you? If this were the case, then you would indeed see and experience life in a whole new way. You would live in a new state of freedom and be able to pursue the will of God with great zeal.

The purpose of this chapter is to explain the purgation that accomplishes just that. This purgation is what Saint John of the Cross calls the *passive night of the senses*. By "passive," he means that it is first and foremost a work of God in your soul. Your responsibility is to simply cooperate with what God wants to do in you.

Your Bodily and Spiritual Natures

In order to understand why this purgation is necessary, and to understand how it will accomplish its purpose, you need to first understand more clearly who you are at your very core, and how the devil, the world and the flesh inflict harm on you on a spiritual level.

As a human being, you are made of both body and spirit. The body is the physical part of who you are but is much more than mere biology. The body also contains within it the ability to sense the world around you and to experience it in your sensory nature. You feel, desire, have human love, see, taste, hear, etc. You encounter the world around you through your five senses and as you do, your passions, emotions and appetites are stirred.

But you also have a purely spiritual part to your nature. Though the body and spirit are intimately intertwined, they are distinct from each other and operate in different ways. For example, when you die (and before you rise again at the end of the world), your body and spirit will separate. When that happens, you will no longer perceive the world through your senses. You will no longer see, hear, touch, smell and taste. But you will still possess the spiritual aspects of your human nature, which includes your intellect, memory and will. Furthermore, your intellect, memory and will have been formed by the sensory information you have received in this life. Therefore, if you have been inordinately attached in your sensory appetites, this knowledge will remain in the spiritual part of your soul. Thus, though the spiritual and sensory parts of your soul are distinct, they are intimately united and interdependent.

What More Needs to be Purged?

Is the person who completes the *active purgation of the senses,* as outlined in the previous chapter, free of all sensory attachments? Well, yes and no. Yes, the person who goes through this first purgation does eliminate all habitual attachments to disordered attachments and desires. But in the process, they became attached to new sensory experiences that they didn't have before. These new sensory experiences must now be purged so that the soul can attach itself to God and God alone in a spiritual way. What are these "new" sensory attachments? They are all of the many good feelings and delights the soul experiences during its Christian journey as a beginner.

Saint John explains that when a soul is a beginner in the life of spiritual development, it is treated by God like a mother caring for a newborn. The mother gives the infant her warm milk, gentle caresses, much affection and the like. But as the child grows, the loving mother holds the child less and less, no longer offers her warm milk, begins to give the child more substantial food and teaches the child to walk. By analogy, God gives the soul all the warm spiritual delights and gentle consolations during the first stage of spiritual development. These spiritual gifts produce many sensory delights, and they are good! The person takes great pleasure in long hours or even whole nights of prayer, penances, fastings, the celebration of the Sacraments and many other spiritual devotions. And just as it is good for an infant to enjoy the comfort of a mother, so it is good for the beginner to delight in the consolations of God. The problem is that the beginner, after nursing on these pleasant delights from God, often becomes more attached to the good feelings and consolations experienced than to God Himself. The beginner is often unaware of the new sensory attachments that are formed as a result of the many spiritual consolations it has received. These new sensory attachments manifest themselves in the Seven Capital Sins now in a new spiritual form.

The purpose of the passive night of the senses is to strip the soul of all spiritual consolations within the sensory part of the soul so that it will be able to be freed from the spiritual sins it has, and thus more easily obtain union directly with God, rather than to be satisfied only with the sensory pleasures that come from God. This purgation will leave the soul loving God, not because of the consolations, but because of love alone. A good spiritual maxim for this stage of spiritual development is as follows: *Learn to love God, not the experience of God.*

The following are examples to help describe the Seven Capital Sins, now in spiritual form:

Spiritual Pride—Spiritual pride is the worst of the spiritual sins, and the "mother" of all of these sins. This sin arises when beginners have certain vain satisfactions and desires that come as a result of their engagement in many spiritual activities. The beginners admire themselves and even see themselves as holier than others. Sometimes they even act like Pharisees who boast of their goodness. The devil knows that all the works they do will lead them to pride. They see the splinter in their brothers' eyes and ignore the logs in their own. They are never satisfied with their confessors, especially if their confessors do not praise them and tell them how great they are. So, they seek out other confessors who do praise them. They are pleased when people praise their holiness. As for their sins, beginners are too embarrassed to confess them honestly, so instead they often communicate to their confessor how good they are rather than how sinful they are. Sometimes they get angry and impatient with themselves when they see their imperfections and faults, thinking they should be a saint already. Beginning souls cannot accept that they are sinners. They beg God to take their imperfections from them, but they pray this way not out of love of God alone, but so that they will not suffer the consequences of their sins. Thus, they often have an imperfect contrition.

Furthermore, beginners do not realize that if God did take their other sins away, this would only increase their pride, which would be worse than continuing to struggle with their present sins! At times, beginners become so fervent for God and for doing good that they become anxious to do more and more. As a result, they fail to see the good that others are doing all around them; they are too consumed with what good they themselves are doing. They only want others to see all the good that they do. And when people don't, beginners get angry.

Spiritual Greed—Beginners are often discontented with the spirituality they have been given by God and always want more. They cannot get enough of spiritual counsels and consolations. They possess many books and spend more time on them than on penance and mortifications. They are obsessed with spiritual objects such as different rosaries and medals, always thinking one is better than another. They are attached to spiritual trinkets, wanting the best and "holiest." These souls do not realize that true devotion must come from the heart. All other "devotions" are nothing other than attachments to spiritual things.

The spiritual greed they experience, then, becomes a sensual desire for spiritual things and experiences. It is difficult for these souls to look beyond the spiritual object or experience so as to see the source: God.

Spiritual Lust—Perhaps surprisingly, impure thoughts of a spiritual nature can arise in the soul, even when the person is deep in prayer or engaged in the Sacraments. These imperfections come from one of three things:

1. The soul takes <u>delight</u> in spiritual things. It is part of human nature that the spiritual and sensual parts of the soul are connected. Therefore, when the spiritual nature takes pleasure in God, the sensual nature seeks pleasure also. However, since the sensual part of the beginner is still imperfect, it displays sensual thoughts and arousals of the flesh that are lustful and impure.

2. The <u>devil</u> also brings these forth when the soul is praying because he does not like prayer. The devil attacks more in prayer than when the soul is not praying. When a soul is in melancholy, and when

it is attacked by the devil, it may not have the strength necessary to overcome it.

3. <u>Fear</u> of these tendencies can also cause a soul to fall deeper into this sin. When the soul is tempted, especially during prayer, it may become shocked and ashamed. This then produces a form of fear that can overwhelm the person and lead to an increased entertainment of these thoughts or even dissuade the person from continuing prayer.

Saint John also explains that some friendships can bring forth feelings of lust. Though some friendships are purely spiritual and are greatly beneficial, some are not. But even a good spiritual friendship can stir up passions in the soul and cause sensual delights. Furthermore, even the memory of that friendship causes sensual experiences. When a soul becomes attached to the good feelings that a friendship produces, a type of spiritual lust may be formed, even if the sensuality is not sexual. In this case, an attachment is formed to the good feelings produced by the good friendship, which makes it difficult for the soul to love God and this person in a detached and holy way. Instead, the soul finds itself wanting more of the good sensual feelings that are received from that friendship.

Spiritual Anger—When beginners experience an end to spiritual pleasure, they often become bitter and want it to return. They are disappointed and become angry. There is no sin in the natural experience of loss, but some allow that experience of loss to turn into a spiritual sin: they become irritated. Some also become irritated with others because of their loss of spiritual consolation. They find themselves wanting to chastise others and portray themselves as images of virtue.

Some beginners also have a good desire for progress in the spiritual life. However, when they find that this is more difficult than they initially thought, they become angry and impatient with themselves. Humorously, Saint John then says that there are others who are so "patient" with spiritual growth that God would like to see them be less patient.

Spiritual Gluttony—This spiritual sin is another one that Saint John spends much time describing. He explains that, because of the sweetness beginners find in spiritual exercises, some are more indulgent in this sweetness they experience than they are in the progress they make or do not make. This is similar to spiritual lust and greed.

Some people fast or do penances to extreme and seek consolation from them. Their only desire is to do that which they want "for God." In the end, they seek spiritual pleasure rather than the will of God. And when they fail to experience sweetness, they think they have not accomplished anything good. They are also very weak in journeying on the hard road of the Cross since they are so attached to sweetness. Their goal must be to become spiritually temperate by submitting *to* God in all things rather than doing what they want *for* God.

Spiritual Envy—These souls are deterred and saddened when they hear others being praised. They cannot bear the praise of others and want to receive the praise themselves. They see some good action of another being acknowledged and immediately think of all that they have done. And when others do not immediately acknowledge what they do, they turn in on themselves with sadness.

Spiritual Sloth—When the beginner is slowly weaned from the spiritual delights and consolation of God, and when the spiritual milk of God dries up, these souls do not only get angry or greedy for more, they become discouraged. They may abandon the way of perfection when God takes pleasure from them, because they want <u>their</u> will rather than God's will. They become, then, spiritually lazy when things do not go as they had planned.

It's not easy to read all that is above, especially when you see some or all of these tendencies within yourself. But do not get discouraged, God is fully aware of your weakness and offers you a cure. You must humbly allow Him to purge you of these spiritual sins so that you will be free to love Him in a more direct way. Only God can help you be purged of these sins through the *passive night of the senses*. Humility, honesty and surrender are key if you are to pass through this purgation.

The spiritual sins mentioned above need to be purged from your soul if you are to discover freedom and are able to arrive at a point of perfect union with God. It is clear that these spiritual manifestations of the Seven Capital Sins come from an attachment to the sensory pleasure one receives from serving God. Therefore, as a beginning soul moves into the stage of proficients, it will be necessary to confront the newly formed spiritual sins by detaching from the sensory delights initially experienced.

The Witness of Cardinal Nguyễn Văn Thuận

One helpful bit of knowledge that should motivate you to allow God to do His cleansing of these sins is that these sins cause tremendous suffering when they remain. This is well illustrated in the life of Cardinal Nguyễn Văn Thuận. Cardinal Thuận was a native of Vietnam and ordained a priest on June 11, 1953. On April 24, 1975 he was appointed Coadjutor Bishop of Saigon. Six days after that appointment, he was arrested by the North Vietnamese and imprisoned in a "reeducation" camp, where he was mostly kept in solitary confinement. He remained there for thirteen years.

His first eight years were spent in a small cell in Nha Trang, an earshot away from the cathedral of his first diocese. Every day he would hear the bells of the cathedral ring and it would cause him great interior suffering. Eventually, he was moved to the reeducation camp in Vinh-Quang where his suffering continued. In his book *Five Loaves and Two Fish*, Cardinal Thuận recalls:

> Many times I was tempted, tormented by the fact that I am 48 years old, the age of maturity; I have worked as a bishop for eight years, I have aquired much pastoral experience, and here I am isolated, inactive, separated from my people, 1700 km away!
>
> One night, I heard a voice prompting me from the depths of my heart: "Why do you torment yourself so? You have to distinguish between God and God's works. Everything you have done and want to continue doing, pastoral visits, formation of seminarians, men and women religious, lay people, youth, building schools, *foyer* for all these students,

missions to evangelize non Christians… all these are excellent works, God's works, but they are not God! If God wants you to abandon all these works, putting them in his hands, do it immediately, and have confidence in Him. God will do it infinitely better than you; he will entrust his works to others who are much more capable than you. You have chosen God alone, not his works![1]

The then bishop, later to be named a cardinal and perhaps one day a saint, made the profound discovery that had already been articulated by Saint John of the Cross several centuries earlier. He discovered that when we serve God, we can often become attached to the "things of God," the joy of the apostolate, the spiritual feelings, and all that brings consolation and joy in our walk as a beginner. But there, in that prison, in solitary confinement for many years, the bishop discovered that his ongoing attachment to the "works of God" was tormenting him. It wasn't the prison itself, the guards or the North Vietnamese government that caused him the most pain. It was his own attachment to something good that was not actually God! Namely, God's works and the pleasure he formerly took in performing those works. This interior discovery gave the bishop a new strength and he was able to begin putting his mind and heart on God alone.

---

[1] François-Xavier Nguyễn Văn Thuận. *Five Loaves and Two Fish*, Copyright © 2000 Lavamis Publishing. Pp. 21-22

Defining the Passive Night of the Senses

The beginner's soul learns to love God, grows in passion for Him, allows the satisfaction obtained in prayer to free itself from many sins and becomes zealous for God and His holy will. This is all good. So, if you are in this stage, this is good! But now it's time to do better. It's time to deepen your relationship with God by being freed of the many "childish" aspects of your spiritual life. Specifically, you must be freed of the spiritual consolations you enjoy so much. Even though they have helped you to grow up until this point, they can take you no further.

At this point, God is going to do most of the work. For your part, you must do the following two main things: 1) <u>Understand</u> what is happening in your soul, and 2) firmly <u>consent</u> to this action of God in your soul. This will happen through the prayer of *purgative contemplation*.

Remember also that, up until this point, the beginner spent much time in *meditation*. That form of prayer was rich in consolation and nourished the soul well for a time. Many holy images and inspirations were received during meditation. But at this next stage of spiritual development, God will dry up the good consolations of meditation and will take on a more active role in your prayer life. And that can hurt! When God, who is all pure and all perfect, enters into your soul, He will immediately begin to "clean house," so to speak. He will especially purify the above-mentioned spiritual sins so that you can love Him in a purer and more spiritual way.

This next step, the *passive night (purgation) of the senses*, is a process of stripping you of all sensory pleasure you receive from spiritual things. God is still just as present to you, and in fact He is even more present, but you will not experience His presence any longer. You will feel dry, abandoned, alone and maybe even initially confused. Your sensory appetites will long to return to the former consolations you enjoyed, but you will not be able to do so, no matter how hard you try. Of course, sometimes God will bring you back to the consolations of meditation, but then take them away again. You may find that this experience goes back and forth for a while between dryness and consolation. When dryness occurs, God is strengthening you, producing a deep spiritual trial within you, testing you, purifying your spiritual desires, and preparing you for a much higher form of union with Him. You will no longer love God only because it feels good to love God; rather, you will have to now love God only because you do love God, even when He feels absent and there is no immediate sensory pleasure in that union.

Discerning the Signs of this Purgation

So how do you know if you are experiencing this passive purgation of your senses? How do you know if what you are actually encountering is the prayer of purgative contemplation and not just dry meditation? How do you know that the "dryness" you feel is not actually on account of depression or even some sin? Saint John gives certain signs to help discern if you are experiencing this purgation, as well as some good pastoral advice on how to more fully consent to this purifying action of God.

He explains that aridity in prayer and in our affection for spiritual things may come from one of two sources:

Source 1: sins, imperfection, weakness, irritable, lukewarmness or bodily disposition

Source 2: passive night of the senses

To discern which of these is the source of your dryness, Saint John offers three principle signs:

Sign 1—When a soul is in the passive night of the senses, it finds no sensory pleasure in things of God, AND it also finds no pleasure in creatures. God does not allow the soul to find attraction or sweetness in anything. Therefore, there is a general loss of sensory satisfaction and delight in everything you used to delight in. Hobbies may be less attractive to you, relationships may not produce the same familiar delight they used to bring, and prayer will become dry and even unpleasant.

Sign 2—The memory is ordinarily centered upon God with much care, concern and attentiveness. As it centers on God, it ponders whether it has offended God since it no longer finds sweetness in anything and wonders if its sins are the reason. In other words, your memory experiences a sort of confusion about this new dryness. To discern this experience, you must consider whether there is *aridity* or if what you actually experience is *lukewarmness*.

Purgative aridity produces strength and determination in your spirit but lukewarmness causes laziness and weakness. When it is purgative aridity you are experiencing, then the senses are weak but the spirit is strong. God transfers the "energy," so to speak, that was formerly found in your senses to your spirit. This is because the sensual part of your soul has no capacity for that which is purely spiritual, and thus your sensual desires and affections remain dry. But as this happens, your spirit grows in pleasure, sweetness and delight.

Your soul may become a bit confused by the *strangeness of the change* that transfers pleasure from the senses to the spirit. You simply must get used to this new experience of pleasure and sweetness in the spirit, but that will take time and purgation. Sometimes you will still long for the nauseating former "food" of the senses and will fail to accept the much sweeter food of the spirit. You may find yourself sitting in a sort of darkness, not able to take pleasure in anything. But if you allow yourself to sit in this purgative contemplation, and remain silent, accepting the fact that all your sensual delight is lost, not thinking of anything or being anxious about anything, then you will begin to experience an inward refreshment that comes from the freedom of the sensual desires, and you will begin to delight in the spiritual ones. In regard to your prayer, when purgative aridity sets in, you must be willing to let go of meditation and no longer rely upon your intellectual reflections as a source of consolation. No reasoning, thinking, memory, or even willing will help. You must simply remain quiet and solitary. God is doing the work alone and you will discover a new peace.

Sign 3—You will no longer be able to meditate using your imagination as you used to do. Your imagination no longer helps prayer, because your sensual inspirations are no longer possible. However, this will not be an absolute experience, meaning that you may go back and forth between periods of meditation and contemplation. God will slowly move you back and forth between these two forms of prayer. At times, you will find that all you can do is sit in silence with an inability to ponder, reflect and meditate. But then you may suddenly find yourself returning to your meditation and reflection for a moment or two. When God does take away your sensory inspirations, you must learn to sit in silence and be fed by God directly while you experience a total aridity in your senses and imagination so that your spirit alone can silently delight in the sweetness of God directly, and not through the imagination, memory, will, etc.

Then Saint John speaks an important line. He says that in this moment "the faculties are suspended." That is, the intellect, memory and will are suspended. The person is no longer able to obtain sensual delights from thinking and willing. Now, the spirit alone receives communications from God directly. Think about that line for a while. If you can understand what that means, then it is a sign that you are understanding Saint John's description of this experience.

Do's and Don'ts of Contemplation

What NOT to do in contemplation—When experiencing the aridity of the senses and the inability to use your intellect, memory and will for meditation on God, you could easily conclude (wrongly) that you are simply not trying hard enough. You may reason that if you just try harder to meditate on God, the sweetness of your prayer will return. You may be tempted to try to regain your former sensual experience in prayer, but this is because you do not realize, at that moment, that God is drawing you higher into a pure spiritual pleasure that is coming directly from God Himself, and not from the thought of God through meditation. As a result, you will experience a sort of fatigue as you try harder and harder. But this is not the right approach..

What you SHOULD do in contemplation—You should simply allow your soul to remain in peace and quiet. It may appear to you that you are actually doing nothing and are wasting time, or that your dryness is the result of weakness or sin, but it's not. Your only goal in this experience of prayer must be to remain silent, allowing God to do what He wants to do. Simply keep yourself in a state of "loving attentiveness" toward God. That's it. Do not try harder. Just remain at peace.

> The way in which they are to conduct themselves in this night of sense is to devote themselves not at all to reasoning and meditation, since this is not the time for it, but to allow the soul to remain in peace and quietness, although it may seem clear to them that they are doing nothing and are wasting their time, and although it may appear to them that it is because of their weakness that they have no desire in that state to think of anything. (*Dark Night,* Book I, Ch. 10)

Saint John then offers an analogy to illustrate his point. He says that if you were posing for a portrait that an artist was painting of you, your only responsibility would be to sit still so that the artist could do his job. If, out of a desire to help the artist, you kept getting up to look at the painting, offering this suggestion or that, you would actually hinder the artist.

God is the artist, and His canvas is your soul. If you want this process to move quickly, then sit silently and allow God to do His work. Do not try to do that which is not your responsibility. Let God do His work in your soul. For your part, merely consent to it and remain lovingly attentive to Him as He works.

This action on God's part is *infused contemplation*. By remaining silent before this act of God, you allow Him to infuse into your soul "yearnings" of love. Those yearnings you experience will be His purifying fire of love as He strips you of your sensual appetites, removes your spiritual sins, and enables you to receive a new and far better spiritual delight.

Two Effects of this Purgative Contemplation

As this enkindling takes place, and as your soul allows itself to be purified of all sensual desires and pleasures, and even from the sensual pleasure and consolation coming from meditation, it suddenly discovers that this is a "happy chance" in that it realizes there is now an opportunity for something so much greater than the former delights of the senses. Therefore, the spirit begins to have "love with yearnings."

The soul then "goes forth" in silence, leaving the sensual part and entering into the spirit. It is free when the night (passive purgation) destroys all sensual pleasures. In place of the former pleasures, the soul begins to obtain numerous virtues and finds a much greater and new form of delight. A spiritual delight in all of these virtues. The former self of the senses dies and the spirit alone lives. And this is a much better state of living.

Blessings of a New Knowing and an Unknowing

If your soul is privileged to enter through this purgation coming from contemplation, you will begin to discover numerous blessings in your life. Those blessings will come in many ways but will begin with the gift of *Spiritual Knowledge* imparted by <u>infused contemplation</u>. As this *new* knowledge is infused by God, you have to go through a process of *unknowing* your former thoughts, ideas, insights and beliefs. It's not that the former knowledge you obtained from your meditations and inspirations was wrong; rather, it wasn't complete and wasn't purified. Now, the new spiritual knowledge God imparts directly to your spirit enlightens you NOT with a knowledge of things *about* God but with a knowledge OF GOD HIMSELF. This is an incredible gift that is only possible by infused contemplation, meaning, you cannot learn this new knowledge by your own effort. You *unknow* and let go of your former infantlike knowledge and come to a deeper understanding of all things in God.

This knowledge will do many things in you. For one, it will give you an authentic realization of your weakness. Perhaps at first you are not sure you want to know that. But if you were to be given that knowledge through infused contemplation, be assured that you would be exceedingly grateful for the new understanding of yourself as God understands you.

Look at it this way. As mentioned earlier, our human nature is composed of two things: body and spirit. The body contains all the senses and the spirit is the intellect, will and memory. Prior to receiving the gift of infused knowledge, you had to rely upon your five senses and all your passions and appetites to teach your mind and direct your will. As a result, your mind often became confused because your senses, passions, appetites and desires are NOT a very reliable source of learning the profound truths of God. In a state of infused contemplation, your intellect and will no longer rely upon your senses, appetites and passions to teach it. Rather, God Himself teaches your spirit (mind and will), and thus the knowledge you gain is far superior to that which you obtained by the sensual inspirations and by the insights you gained by your senses, meditations, sensual inspirations and the like.

As for gaining a new understanding of your weakness, it's as if your spirit is now able to look at your sensory appetites in your body and suddenly realizes how poor a guide they have been. That realization includes a clear understanding that your passions, affections and desires are greatly disordered and are hard to tame. This is what St. Paul is speaking of when he says, "Miserable one that I am! Who will deliver me from this mortal body?" (Romans 7:24) He realized his wretchedness, lowliness and weakness by receiving the gift of knowledge from infused contemplation. Before this new knowledge of your weakness, the sweetness of your many consolations hid the true depth of your wretchedness, but now you see yourself more clearly. Why is this good? Because it is a fuller sharing in the Truth of who you are. In this case, the realization of your wretchedness will not leave you depressed. Rather, it will leave you with incredible gratitude because you simultaneously see your wretchedness in the light of God's mercy. You are more clearly aware of how much God has done for you. And you are more easily, by God's grace, able to be freed of your powerful and controlling disordered appetites and desires.

Spiritual Humility Flows—By a special grace, you will no longer be deluded to think highly of yourself. Again, this is simply seeing yourself in the light of Truth. All of the former sensual pleasure you received from meditation and spiritual sweetness left you with the earlier mentioned sin of spiritual pride. Now, the humble truth of who you are is made clear, and spiritual pride is eliminated. Spiritual humility allows you to grow in self-knowledge, and the self-knowledge is that you realize you can do nothing by yourself without God. This is good because you are freed of all false hope of doing great things by yourself and you begin to see only your inability and weakness. As a result, your hope is now in God, and you see that God is the one doing great things in you. You will begin to learn to relate with God in a new way and to treat God with a much greater reverence. As a result, you obey God on a new level and more easily attribute all good things to God rather than to yourself.

Furthermore, you will realize that all you obtained in your prayer of meditation as a beginner is nothing compared to the reality of who God is. You realize that the former insights coming from both meditation and the senses are darkness compared to the spiritual knowledge you gain by this new form of infused contemplation.

All Other Spiritual Sins are Eliminated—Spiritual Pride is the mother of all spiritual sins. Therefore, as spiritual humility grows, so also every other spiritual sin is eliminated, and their contrary spiritual virtue takes their place. Perhaps you would find it helpful at this time to return to the earlier list of the seven spiritual capital sins and consider how this contemplative purgation frees you from each.

Fear of God—"Fear" of God may not be a concept that you are used to seeing as good. But it is a great gift to obtain. When you are given a holy fear of God, you are not frightened by God; rather, you have a new spiritual desire to make sure you never lose the presence of God in your life. Therefore, you become aware that your former sins kept you from this deep state of union with God, and thus you become zealous to never fall into those sins again lest you lose the closeness you have with God. Holy fear also fires your soul with such a love of God that you never want to offend God, simply because you love Him. This holy fear is of great benefit.

Various Virtues—Patience and long suffering are produced. The aridity and lack of consolation you have gone through in your sensory appetites will help you grow in prayer and contemplation, producing patience so that you can more easily endure long suffering, no matter what that suffering entails. You begin to practice the "charity of God" because you no longer are motivated only by the sweetness of your experience of God. Instead, you are now only motivated by the pure love of God. As a result, fortitude is formed, and you become much stronger in the practice of the virtues. In the end, you discover that in your weakness (that is, in the experience of aridity and dryness), you become strong. Chapter Six offers an examination of conscience that may be helpful to review that presents both the Seven Capital Sins as well as their contrary virtues. The Seven Capital Virtues are especially helpful to ponder in more detail at this point.

Bondage is Eliminated—The soul then begins to sing "Oh happy chance, I went forth without being observed." This poetic expression means that you are freed from the bondage and subjection of the desires and affections of the sensory appetites without being observed, bound or influenced by the world, the devil or the flesh. Recall the first section of this chapter when it was said that the ultimate goal of this purgation was to free you from the influence of these three things: the flesh, the devil and the world.

Natural Passions of the Soul—*Joy, hope, grief* and *fear* are what Saint John defines as the natural passions of your soul. These passions were formerly confused and disordered. The devil, the flesh and the world wreaked havoc upon them, misleading you through their disorder. Now, these passions are ordered and benefit you in a new way. Joy is now joy in God alone. Hope is hope in God alone. Grief no longer beats you down. And fear no longer controls you. These natural passions of the lower part of the soul are calmed by aridity. Thus, as the poem says, "My house is now at rest."

These natural passions are very good sources of self-examination. If you find these passions in you, especially if they have great power over you, then pay attention to them. For example, if you find yourself regularly overwhelmed by fear, God wants to free you from that through this prayer of contemplation. If you are always seeking joy in lowly and passing things, such as the world or the flesh, then know that this prayer of contemplation is the cure. If you are always hoping in this thing or that, and especially if you are obsessed with some self-conceived hope, even if you think it is God's will, then it's time to let it go. God will accomplish His will in you if you let Him. Too often we presume we know what is best and we work with great anxiety to do what is, in truth, our will and not God's. And if grief weighs heavy upon you for any reason whatsoever, let God enter in and lift that heavy burden. The prayer of contemplation is the answer to all of these passions of the soul when they are excessive and disordered.

The Final Test through Trial and Temptations

As you begin to experience the many blessings of this purgation, and as your soul begins to be "at rest" from the former disorders and attachment to your sensual appetites, you will have to endure, sometimes for many years, strong trials and temptations. This is so that God can complete the good work He has begun in you and bring it to completion.

Saint John identifies three main trials people go through but also makes it clear that these are not absolute to every person. Some will experience many other trials, and some will not experience the three he mentions to a serious degree. So, the key is to be aware that trials and temptations will come. But if you know this, then you will be in a good position to continually overcome them and, by God's grace, complete this purgation of your sensory appetites. The three temptations that Saint John mentions are as follows:

The Spirit of Fornication—This demonic spirit may be allowed to tempt you, in a very vile way, with strong images and desires for sensual pleasure. Though this will involve disordered sexual temptations, it is not exclusive to those specific temptations. Recall that spiritual lust involves not only sexual desires but also a lust for all sensual attractions.

The Spirit of Blaspheme—This demonic spirit will tempt you in the area of the things of God. You may struggle with a strong urge to doubt what God has done in your life, what He continues to do and what He promises to do in the future. This is an attack upon faith and on all that you are coming to know through the gift of infused knowledge.

The Spirit of Confusion—Saint John says that this is one of the most painful spirits to endure. When tempted and afflicted by this spirit, you may find yourself filled with almost unbearable scrupulosity. You may find yourself analyzing everything in your life to an intense degree. When you seek counsel from others, it produces little or no help. You find yourself confused about even the most minute detail of life. Faith and trust in God, attentiveness to His voice and total surrender will enable you to endure and overcome these temptations.

If your soul is not tried, tested and tempted by these and other vile spirits, you cannot grow strong in virtue. Thus, the end goal of God allowing these afflictions is virtue. Very strong virtue. If this is difficult for you, look at these temptations from the point of view of the end result they produce rather than the struggle that is endured as they are afflicted upon you. Affliction produces strength, and the greater the affliction, the stronger you will become.

And don't worry, God knows exactly how much you can endure. Those who are strong, God purges quickly by afflicting them intensely. Those who are weak, God moves slowly, permitting only slight temptations, giving also regular sensual consolations to make sure they do not fail these trials. And for the weakest souls, Saint John says that God guides them personally by regularly appearing to them, then moving away, then coming again to keep them from turning away completely.

The End Result

The end result of passing through this *passive night of the senses* is freedom, virtue and a pure love of God. As you pass through this purgation, you enter into what is traditionally called the "Illuminative Way," the "Way of Proficients," or the "Way of Infused Contemplation."

In this spiritual state, life is incalculably more glorious than your former state. You love in purity, not in selfishness. You have a new knowledge of God Himself, not just knowledge of the ways of God. God speaks directly to you, not through images and ideas. You live guided by the Spirit of God, not by your own good effort.

Chapter Three

Growing in Illumination through Contemplation

The Active Night of the Spirit

STOP it!

There is good news in this chapter for those who have particular struggles. Specifically, if you are one who tends to obsess in your thoughts, overanalyze, act with scrupulosity, or weary yourself with trying to live God's will, then this chapter is especially for you! One simple and straightforward message that could be gained is "STOP it!" Stop overthinking. Stop overanalyzing. Stop causing yourself undue anxiety about spiritual things. Stop being scrupulous. And stop thinking so much about yourself!

This is important because sometimes those who seek spiritual perfection end up trying too hard when, in truth, they need to try less hard and stop imposing excessive spiritual, mental and emotional burdens on themselves. Sometimes they need to simply trust in God more and rely upon themselves less.

Additionally, this chapter will present the virtues of faith, hope and charity as they are infused into the soul by God through the prayer of contemplation. Understanding these infused virtues will help to clarify how the soul can properly dispose itself to receive them more fully. With that said, this chapter will present to us the next step of purgation necessary for perfection: The Active Night of the Spirit.

General Overview

At this point of spiritual development, you must prepare yourself to receive the sustained prayer of infused contemplation rather than return to the former prayer of meditation, because you need more than what meditation, reflection, thinking and reasoning can offer. You need God in His pure form. This is possible only by allowing infused contemplation to become *habitual*. Though this *infused* contemplation will not become perfected and habitual until the next stage of spiritual development, in the *passive night of the spirit*, the soul must begin to become more disposed to this prayer during this stage of the *active* night of the spirit.

We already spoke about how the prayer of contemplation is purgative of the sensual spiritual appetites, freeing a person from spiritual sins (spiritual pride, gluttony, sloth, etc.) and filling the soul with countless virtues. Now we must see how infused contemplation must continue to grow and completely reform the intellect, memory and will. The new knowledge that is imparted by infused faith continues to grow, a new direction in life is more completely given by infused hope, and a new love of God and neighbor is strengthened by infused charity.

Analogies never suffice to present the clear picture, but let's use one to try to illustrate this change. Let's say you are in school to become a nurse. You spend your first three years studying in class and at home, learning all ABOUT nursing. You learn the language, the theories, and much more. But learning about nursing cannot make you a nurse. Therefore, in your final year of nursing school you enter into a practicum and actually do the work of a nurse. All you learned in school helps you, but actually functioning as a nurse makes it real. There is a new knowledge given through the act of being a nurse. And even though your former lessons at school helped prepare you for this point, unless you are willing to learn in a new way, through practical experience, you will forever remain a "theoretical" nurse and not a real one.

So it is with this new stage of spiritual development. All you've learned up until now in your spiritual development is of great value. But it's not enough to enter into perfect union with God. What you must do now is embrace "on the job training," so to speak, which will be accomplished through ongoing infused contemplation. A new depth of faith, hope and charity must become habitually present in your spirit to a profound degree. Your former gifts of faith, hope and charity must deepen, become purified and be transformed. This happens as you learn to "pray always" and are led by the Spirit of God every hour of the day, every day of the week! Once infused contemplation becomes a perpetual habit (during the *passive* night of the spirit), you will be drawn into the depths of the spiritual marriage with God, that is, divine union.

In order to allow faith, hope and charity to become habitually infused into your intellect, memory and will, it is essential that you understand what *infused* faith, *infused* hope and *infused* charity are and how they are communicated to you by God in their purest forms. During the active night of the spirit, the soul prepares itself for these gifts by eliminating various obstacles to the reception of these three infused virtues. Henceforth, we will look at what happens as these three virtues are infused into the soul, and then we will look at the *active* part of this process, meaning, that which you can do to help it take place.

Pure Infused Faith and the Intellect

At first, as a soul goes through an initial conversion and begins to live a stable Christian life, it learns much about God. This process of discovering many truths about God is exciting, inspiring, consoling and encouraging. As the person prays and meditates upon the truths that God has revealed, the new interior discoveries of faith spark much enthusiasm for the Christian walk with Christ. The soul begins to change its life, goes through the initial detachment from habitual sins and worldly attachments, and allows its newfound relationship with God to bring stability and clarity to its life.

Often times, this stage of spiritual development lasts for many years. The Christian learns to be selfless, caring, evangelistic and faithful, doing many things for God and for others. The person becomes very familiar with the teachings of Christ, the Church, the Gospels and the lives of the saints.

Traditionally, this stage of spiritual development is called the "Illuminative Way" and is a very stable and comfortable way of life. Within this state, as God begins to call the soul deeper, and as the person continues to discover that prayer is not as consoling as it initially was, <u>perseverance is essential</u>. As it presses on through those periods, the soul becomes stronger and more committed to God. The loss of spiritual consolation enables the soul to pray and believe in God NOT because it feels like doing so, but because of something much deeper. The soul's knowledge of God becomes purified as faith is more directly infused by God.

The clearest sign of the soul's deepening relationship with God is the dryness it experiences in prayer and in its perseverance in works of charity. It may also find that its faith begins to change from being exceptionally clear and passionate, to being a bit more obscure and less passionate. This is because faith is moving from knowledge *about* God to knowledge *of* God Himself. As the intellect becomes infused with the gift of faith, it begins to discover that God is beyond what it can figure out. God cannot be "solved." The soul's former knowledge about the many aspects of God's life begins to be less and less clear, less visual, less particular, less sensory. In place of this, the soul begins to be given a more <u>general</u> knowledge of God Himself on a spiritual level, but it is a knowledge that is more certain than before because it is being directly infused by God rather than through the use of concepts or ideas gained through the senses. As a result, the soul grows in confidence and attains a much broader understanding of God. However, this is a knowledge the soul cannot explain as before with the use of sensory concepts and forms.

This is because God cannot be fully understood by the human mind using rational deductions. Therefore, as you do begin to know Him more deeply, you will actually go through an experience of feeling as if you know Him less clearly. The more you come to know the INFINITE God, the more you realize that HE IS infinite, incomprehensible, unknowable, and amazing beyond what you could ever fathom. This discovery of God in a new and more pure way leaves the soul humble, and the knowledge, though greater, is actually more obscure. Therefore, Saint John says that faith causes a sort of "darkness" in the intellect. Not in a negative way, but in a humble discovery of the infinite.

To illustrate, imagine if you wanted to learn about the Sun. As a result, you have your pupils dilated so that you can take in more of the Sun. Then, you go outside on a very sunny day and you attempt to spend an hour gazing directly into the Sun. What would the result of such an exercise be? You'd blind yourself. Your pupils could not contain the brightness of the Sun in its pure form. It's too much.

So it is with the human intellect. As God is perceived in His more pure form, as a result of Him directly infusing knowledge of Himself into your intellect through infused contemplation, your intellect is blinded, darkened, and overwhelmed at the infinite mystery of God. But what needs to be understood at this point is that, unlike staring directly at the Sun, infused contemplation of God does not harm your intellect; it enlightens it, illumines it, and strengthens it. But in this experience of infused faith, there is a darkening of all former knowledge *about* God so that you can begin to know God Himself.

To further our analogy, imagine if you were given a special grace in that you COULD encounter the full splendor of the Sun in a new way. Imagine if its heat did not harm you and its brightness did not blind you. Then imagine if you could be transported to the Sun to see and touch it up close. You study the various spots, you enter into its very center, you examine everything about it. That would be AMAZING! And that is what God wants to do with you! He wants you to encounter Him in His pure form. But to do that, your natural intellect must be transformed so that you can know the very essence of God. This takes time. But you will know that you know God more certainly, while at the same time the knowledge will be more general, less specific, and experienced as a darkening of all former knowledge.

Pure Infused Hope and the Memory

Persons who have moved from the state of beginner to proficient, and who are now living in the Illuminative Way, will have many wonderful memories of God in the form of spiritual concepts. They will have many memories of all that God has done in their lives. Their memory of all they have learned, experienced, hoped, and discovered will greatly affect who they are and will be integral to their human personality.

In addition to the many good and spiritual memories they have of God, of prayer and their experiences within the Christian life, each person carries many other natural memories, and even sinful ones. The past hurts, joys, labor, relationships, activities and so on, leave impressed upon the memory countless experiences. Some good, some not so good.

Our memory has a direct effect upon our <u>hope</u>. Saint John explains that hope focuses upon that which we <u>do not</u> possess. Therefore, he goes on to explain that the more we "possess" within our memory, the less will be our hope in God. The more we hold on to, reflect upon, ponder and think about in an earthly way, the less we will be able to have a pure hope in God.

When our memories are very alive and active, our hopes will be based upon the many things we have learned about God and life (good or bad) over the years. When we have learned that God is faithful and guides us through difficult times, we may more easily trust Him when new hardships arise. And in that case, one's hope is based on their past experience of God's fidelity in their life. And that is good for the beginner, but dangers will eventually arise as the soul strives for perfection.

Additionally, even the proficient who has had many other natural experiences, and sinful ones, will often be tempted to reflect upon those experiences over and over. Thus, Saint John explains that in both the active night of the spirit and even more so in the passive one, the memory must go through a process of "forgetting" so that it no longer "possesses" all of its past experiences, be they sin, natural experiences or even spiritual ones.

Forgetting the evils and worldly experiences of life may be easy for many to accept as a wise goal. It is clear that many of those memories lead to anger, division, obsessive thinking, other sins and the like. Some will even waste a tremendous amount of time and energy dwelling upon the past.

But what about "forgetting" the good spiritual experiences of one's life? Why would this be wise? Saint John explains that just as infused faith leads a soul to move from knowing much *about* God to a purer knowledge *of* God, so also infused hope has a similar effect upon the memory. When hope is divinely infused into one's memory, the soul no longer relies upon all its past experiences and knowledge of God as the basis of its hope. It no longer has to come up with its own "good" ideas for the future. Instead, the soul suddenly begins to have something better. It has direction from God Himself rather than from its own process of intellectual reasoning based on past ideas and experiences. Since it lets go of its possession of these spiritual ideas, the memory becomes "poor," so to speak. But it is only in this poverty that hope can be born. Hope has as its focus that which one does not possess, and that which one does not see. "Faith is the realization of what is hoped for and evidence of things not seen" (Hebrews 11:1).

It may sound strange that infused hope has the effect of causing a soul to begin to <u>forget</u> all of its past ideas of God, its past insights, revelations, experiences, and other forms of knowledge about God. But unless knowledge *about* God begins to fade and is no longer the basis for hope, then pure infused hope (that which we do not see) cannot help direct the soul to the unknown will of God in the most perfect way.

This is why, in the beginning of this chapter, it was mentioned that those who overanalyze, overthink, act with scrupulosity and find themselves anxious about many things are in for some good news. The good news is that they can STOP trying to figure everything out. They can begin by letting go of their attachment to all past memories that are harmful and of no use on their journey to divine union. There are many things we are tempted to remember that are best forgotten. Even normal daily activities should be recalled only so as to fulfill one's duty. When the duty is done, the memory should return to God with exclusive focus.

Furthermore, as the soul seeks to move forward fulfilling the will of God, it should seek to set aside its own self-created hopes and begin to let God and God alone be the source of hope. The overthinkers will suddenly discover that they do hope in God, but with a hope that is not based on some long and complex process of thinking and reasoning based on all they remember about God. Nor is it based upon what they think is best, namely, THEIR idea of God's plan. Instead, this new hope is pure and infused. It's just there. The soul then discovers a new repose, confidence and conviction. Like faith, this gift of hope is somewhat obscure, not based on a series of logical conclusions. It's based only on the presence of God in their lives, instilling hope in Him alone.

Pure Infused Charity and the Will

The beginner in the Christian life will have to make choice after choice in favor of love rather than selfishness. The soul will hear the Word of God, be inspired to act according to God's law, examine its own actions and try to change its sinful ways. This is so that the soul's actions more clearly conform to the love of God. This is the stage of charity in the beginner. As the soul begins to act with charity, making one good decision after another, it experiences great delight in what it does. As a result, it loves being used by God. Charity becomes the soul's spiritual food and it inspires the soul to love even more.

However, God will eventually begin to purify the person's will by infusing charity into the will in a process beyond that of mere beginners. The good feelings, consolations and delights become less and less the motivating force behind what the person does. Instead, God begins to infuse charity directly into a person's will, and the soul begins to love in God and by God rather than out of its own personal reasoning flowing from consoling motivations.

This process of growing in infused charity is not only fascinating, it's awe-inspiring. Therefore, let's look more clearly at the difference between charity in the life of the beginner, and infused charity in the life of the proficient and perfect.

Initially in the Christian life, a person's will is often motivated by its inspired passions and emotions. As God and His will are discovered by the beginner, there is an excitement in the sensory part of a person's soul, and that excitement is a true motivation. Other motivating factors for one's will are the natural passions already mentioned of hope, sorrow and fear.

When a person begins to live in this higher state, as a proficient, charity begins to be infused directly into the will, and not through the passions. The *passions* of joy in serving God and more natural hope for doing great things for God begin to fade. Additionally, natural sorrow and fear also affect the person less. As a result, the person's will is no longer directed by the passions, not even the good passions. Instead, God's divine will itself infuses charity into one's will, and thus the divine will becomes the one and only motivating source of a person's charity.

But it doesn't stop there! As charity is directly infused into a person's will, and God alone directs their actions, they begin to discover that God's will, acting upon them, also begins to take hold of their passions and directs them. So it's a sort of complete reversal. At first, the natural passions (joy, hope, fear, sorrow) influenced and directed the will. Now, infused charity alone directs the will and the person's will then directs its passions, tempers them and uses them for love of God and others.

Preparing for HABITUAL Contemplation

At this point, you may be wondering what your role is in this process of receiving infused faith, hope and charity. Well, you do have an essential role. That role could be summarized as actively and consciously *getting out of the way!*

Often times, as a soul begins to experience God entering its life in this new and infused way, the soul may feel that things are awkward, strange, new and confusing. As a result, the soul often interferes with the infused action of God and hinders His ability to transform its mind, memories and will. Therefore, here is some practical advice on how you can get out of the way and allow God to work in you.

Faith—When God begins to infuse faith into your intellect, don't fight it. When this infused contemplation begins, you may sense that you need to sit silently more than to try to meditate or think. You will begin to discover that all that you formerly knew about God is nothing compared to God Himself. As a result, actively begin to let go of your former ideas of God. It's not that they were wrong; they were just incomplete. Recall the words of Saint Paul as he went through this process of discovering pure infused faith:

> For we know partially and we prophesy partially, but when the perfect comes, the partial will pass away. When I was a child, I used to talk as a child, think as a child, reason as a child; when I became a man, I put aside childish things. At present we see indistinctly, as in a mirror, but then face to face. At present I know partially; then I shall know fully, as I am fully known. (1 Corinthians 13:9-12)

Saint Paul was in the process of moving from childish ways, seeing only partially, to becoming a spiritual adult and seeing more clearly.

Therefore, the best practical advice that can be given in regard to growing in infused faith is simply "let it happen." You can't force it to happen, you can only dispose yourself to let God do it in you. In fact, you may end up even stopping it altogether by interfering in the process. So, get out of the way and let the transformation happen when God begins to give you this gift. Let God communicate Himself to you in this new and deeper way when He chooses to do so. When you begin to experience this, don't be surprised if it seems strange. Don't be afraid to let go of your former knowledge of

God. As faith is infused, you will have to go through a whole new process of knowing. Your formal ideas, concepts, understanding and insights about God will fade, and you will begin to know God in a new, general, obscure but deeply certain way. You will begin to "gaze upon the Sun" and experience a certain level of blindness and darkness in your natural intellect as a result. But the light you do receive into your spirit will change you, without you even having to figure out how. Think less, surrender more.

Hope—Similarly to the infusion of faith, when God wants to infuse pure hope into your memory, let Him. The way you do that is by letting go of YOUR own self-conceived hopes. In other words, don't come up with ideas, imaginations, plans, ambitions, etc., in life and base your hopes for the future on your past experiences of God. That's all fine, for the beginner. However, now as a proficient in the Illuminative Way, you will be called to hope in a higher way. The memory must go through a process of forgetting all past sin, natural knowledge and even spiritual knowledge. With the latter, it's not that the past spiritual ideas and hopes you had are bad. Rather, they are not as perfect as they could be. As a result, God wants to lead you directly and He wants you to "forget" much of what you learned up until now.

The best thing you can do in this process is to rest, be silent, let God take over and take control of not only your past but also your present and future. You no longer have to figure everything out. You no longer have to analyze all that you have done. You no longer have to set the course for your future. God will do that, and He will lead you one step at a time. Thus, divinely infused hope is very freeing to the soul and lifts many heavy burdens that come from human and worldly joys, hopes, sorrows and fears.

Charity—When charity begins to be infused, you will begin to see a complete reordering of the way your passions and will work. You will no longer be motivated to love out of a passion for God or others. Instead, your motivation will come from God alone. As a result, your will must be purified. It may feel awkward to allow God to motivate you rather than your passions. In order to let God do this in you, you must be willing to let your passions become stilled, quiet and at rest. When you do, and when God becomes the pure source of your charity, you will see your passion return in a new way. You will see that your will, now possessed by the will of God, controls your passions and not the reverse any longer. Your will <u>will</u> be in charge of your actions and your will <u>will</u> be directed by the pure and infused love of God. You will have new strength to love heroically, deeply and unwaveringly.

As for your responsibility, you must allow this transition to take place. You must allow your passions to die down so that they can later rise up again under the control of your will. You must seek to surrender to the will of God so that He and He alone is in control of your life. This surrender must, at first, be very intentional on your part. But as you consent, God will take over and complete this transformation in love.

Patient endurance—One last bit of practical advice is that the soul must learn to persevere through all forms of suffering and must grow to a profound degree in the virtue of patient endurance. The transformation of your intellect, memory and will is not easy and will often be accompanied by suffering. Suffering my come through interior dryness, intense temptations, trials, and humiliations. But these struggles are necessary so that the soul can "pass the test," so to speak, and become strong in virtue. Patient endurance will grow as one's prayer is transformed into the infused contemplation spoken of thus far and will be perfected only through the final *passive* purification of the spirit spoken of in the next chapter.

As You Pray…

Though the person in this stage of spiritual development, that of the proficient, will be regularly drawn into contemplation and will need to abandon former practices of meditation, there will be times when it is necessary to pray a certain way, and even to begin a certain meditation. Below is a good prayer written by Saint Ignatius of Loyola that can be used at this stage, since it seeks to surrender one's mind, memory and will.

> Take, Lord, and receive all my liberty,
> my memory, my understanding,
> and my entire will,
> All I have and call my own.
> You have given all to me.
> To you, Lord, I return it.
> Everything is yours; do with it what you will.
> Give me only your love and your grace,
> that is enough for me.
> Amen.

In addition to this prayer, it is helpful to seek three things as you begin your prayer:

Growing in Illumination Through Contemplation

1. Seek to plunge your mind into the obscurity and blindness of pure faith. A good image for this would be to see God, with your mind's eye, as pure light, brighter than the Sun itself, shining down upon you. The brightness is so overwhelming that it blinds you of all other knowledge you have of God. His brightness is all you see.

2. Seek to forget all you remember about God. You will be tempted, time and time again, to think about God rather than to just pray. You will be tempted to go through various reasoning processes, trying to put together various pieces of your life. Forget it. Let it all go. Seek to have an empty memory so that God can fully possess your memory alone with His pure self and gift of infused hope.

3. Seek to let go of every choice you need to make. Detach from every preference, every spiritual desire, everything you "think" God wants of you. Instead, simply rest in His will. Wait on Him. When He is ready, He will guide you at the right time in the right way. Only if you allow God to strip your will of all your own decisions and preferences can God fully possess your will with His.

Chapter Four

A Third Conversion

The Passive Night of the Spirit

The Power of a Cocoon

Think about the amazing transformation that takes place as a caterpillar enters a cocoon. Once inside that still and dark place, it is transformed into a new creation. Its DNA remains the same. It is still the same creature. But it emerges transformed, entirely new.

The Passive Night of the Spirit could be likened to entering a cocoon. The reason this must happen is that God wants to recreate you *for a third time!* True, when you initially go through Baptism, turn from sin and become a Christian, you are made new. This is your first conversion. Sanctifying grace enters your life and you begin to walk as a child of God. As you grow in your Christian life, God will bring you through the active and passive purgation of your senses and draw you into the life of a proficient, which is the Illuminative Way. This could be termed your *second conversion.* But as you grow and mature in the Christian life as a proficient, you should anticipate the full metamorphosis of your life into the creation God intends. That metamorphosis culminates in Christian perfection. And Christian perfection is obtained once God brings you through this last dark and painful purgation of your spirit. It is painful because everything not of God and His will must be completely stripped away and utterly annihilated. The soul at this stage is ready to go through its third and final conversion, which is essentially a transitional phase culminating into divine union.

The Goal of the Passive Night of the Spirit

This *passive* purgation of the spirit is the most transformative of all! It's also the most painful of them all. But the end does justify the means. This purgation of the spirit does three main things to the soul for three main reasons.

1. This purgation brings <u>darkness</u> to the spirit (the intellect, memory and will)—*so that* the soul can ultimately be fully illuminated by God and given light in EVERYTHING.
2. This purgation leaves the spirit <u>miserable</u> and <u>humbled</u> in its natural state—*so that* the soul can be exalted and raised up further than it could ever imagine.
3. This purgation <u>impoverishes</u> the soul, <u>emptying</u> it of all natural attachment and affection—*so that* it may be divinely stretched forward to bear the richest new fruit in all things both in Heaven and on Earth.

The spirit must become simple, pure and detached from all things, losing natural affection for all things *so that* the soul can become divinely united to all things, natural and supernatural, and live in the purest love imaginable. The spirit, through its purity, will now have the pure sweetness of all good things. The perfected person will enjoy the taste, smell, touch, sight and sound of all things more perfectly and with perfect delight. They will discover the divine beauty and joy of all relationships as God enjoys them. They will love God in a selfless way, receiving Him as a pure and holy gift to the soul. And they will share in all the delights in the heart of God Himself.

The Painful Purgation One Goes Through

To obtain all that was just mentioned, the soul must be completely *annihilated* in its former and lower self. This will be painful, because the soul will be radically and completely transformed. Change will hurt. New understanding reveals painful truths. The pure light of God is blinding and overwhelming. The tiniest root of every sin is removed. The soul then experiences confusion on the deepest level. In general, the purgation follows a series of typical transformative stages.

First, when divine light floods the soul, the soul sees all things more clearly. One thing that is seen is its sin. It's like taking a bright light and shining it under a sofa and being made aware of the dirt that has accumulated. When God's light shines in your soul, you will see everything that is contrary to that light. This is a painful realization and leaves the soul, at times, with a complete realization of its miserable state. Seeing every sin leaves the soul realizing that it is incapable, by itself, of ever attaining perfection. But this <u>humiliating</u> realization is necessary if the soul is to abandon all hope in itself, and receive the pure faith, hope and charity given by God.

Second, as the soul sees its wretchedness, meaning every imperfection brought to light, it cannot imagine that it could be loved by anyone. It feels its misery and weakness and, like Job, feels as if its proper place is to sit on the dunghill, abandoned by God and by all. Thus, its human hope is vanquished. And that hurts.

Third, as the soul observes God entering it more deeply, taking possession of it, the soul realizes that it must die. The old man, the sinful man, the deep roots of every attachment, must be destroyed. This realization of total annihilation is painful and shocking to the soul. It's as if, in the cocoon, the soul is watching its old self be destroyed. Though its subsequent emergence is ultimately glorious, there is still a pain associated with the death of the old self.

Fourth, as the soul experiences the pain of this purgation and receives this newly-infused knowledge from God, it is tempted to despair, realizing that it will never be able to enjoy life as it once did. This is because the soul cannot yet see through this darkness and gaze upon that which awaits it. Instead, it looks back to the past, wishing it could regain its former joys and sensory affections that it once experienced from its spiritual encounters. Upon realizing it will never return as it was, the soul feels a selfish sorrow and pain.

Fifth, the soul experiences a wearisome restlessness, having yearnings for God. But its experience is that God is gone, nowhere to be found. The soul seeks spiritual consolation, but it finds none. The sensory experience of

God, the former imperfect knowledge of God, the former imperfect clarity of God's will, leaves the soul. As a result, the soul initially feels hopeless and alone. This purgation is necessary so that the soul can eventually be kindled by the fire of God's infused faith, hope and love alone, in a new and direct way.

Lastly, the soul can no longer pray as it once did. When it tries to pray, it seems as if its prayers are unheard. Thus, the soul experiences a total death to the way it used to communicate with God. But this is necessary if it is to come to pray in a new way. However, the initial experience includes a <u>feeling</u> of loss of the precious gift of prayer, even though its prayer is actually much deeper.

Analogy of a Log and Fire

Saint John uses the image of a log being placed on a fire to teach us about this final purgation. If you've ever sat around a campfire and watched as a new log was placed on a blazing fire, you will understand the lesson he teaches. At first, the log begins to crackle. This is because there are impurities in the log, such as moisture and sap, that cannot properly take on the nature of fire. Those impurities must be burnt out. Also, the log becomes blackened before it catches fire. Eventually, when all the impurities are gone, the log actually takes on the properties of the fire all the way to its center, in that it glows, gives heat and is beautiful as it becomes one with the flame. And once transformed by fire, the fire cannot be separated from the burning log. The flame and log are one.

So it is with the soul. It must first be purged of all impurities. As this happens, it becomes "blackened," making it appear unsightly and dirty to itself. But as the purgation takes place by the blazing flame of God's love, the soul begins to take on the nature of the divine Spirit. God's light and heat radiate. Thus, the divine presence that the soul is to be transformed into first has the effect of purging it by its ever-closening presence. God's divinely infused presence at first burns, purges and reveals its misery and sin until the soul is enkindled and transformed. It takes a long time for the innermost part of the soul to be purified and enkindled, but once this happens, the soul and God are one.

This innermost purgation of the soul takes place by divine love. The soul grows deeper and deeper in love of God, and it is this deepening love that purges it. The intellect remains darkened and unable to see God clearly, but love begins to enkindle the will in a new and transforming way. Love is infused, and this love purges as it grows.

Five Degrees of Love

It may be helpful now to look at a brief summary of five different degrees of love that a soul encounters. Saint John describes these degrees within various chapters of the *Dark Night of the Soul* as follows:

1. Sensory feelings of fervor (*Dark Night* 1.1.2)
2. A dry concern about serving God (*Dark Night* 1.11.2)
3. A sensory enkindling of love (*Dark Night* 1.11.1)

4. An admiring and esteeming love (*Dark Night* 2.13.5)
5. Enkindling with an impassioned love in the spirit (*Dark Night* 2.11.1-5; 13.3-9)

Let's begin by briefly reviewing the first four degrees of love. This will provide us with the necessary context to understand a new degree of love that has not yet been covered (#5 above).

Sensory feelings of fervor—This first degree of love is best captured by the image of a mother nursing her newborn. The baby is quite content with this milk and takes delight in it. The "milk" for the soul is found in the apostolic works, long nights in prayer, penances, sacraments, and spiritual conversations. It provides a sensory delight (meaning emotional consolation) given by God to the beginner. Saint John uses the following Scripture passage to illustrate how one loves in this first, sensory degree: "like newborn infants, long for pure spiritual milk so that through it you may grow into salvation, for you have tasted that the Lord is good" (1 Peter 2:2-3).

A dry concern about serving God—In the second degree of love, the soul is given the gift of "fear of the Lord." The consolations in the sensory appetites that were experienced in the first degree of love of God are dried up, but now the soul begins to experience a great concern about serving God and never offending Him. Though the soul feels dry and void in its sensory part, it is attentive to God. The soul no longer serves God because it feels good; rather, it serves because of a grace given to it, which drives it to serve God in a purer way. Though this does not "feel" as delightful as the first degree of love, it is of a higher nature nonetheless.

A sensory enkindling of love—This third degree of love enkindles the soul with a new desire to serve God. Not only does it never want to offend God (fear of the Lord), it also thirsts more for God Himself, to possess Him and serve Him. Even though there is a great thirst to love and serve God, the soul is not aware of *why* it thirsts. It only knows *that it does* thirst. This thirst is on the sensory level of the soul rather than in the spirit, and the thirst is so strong that the soul feels like it is dying of a hunger that cannot be satisfied. Saint John refers to the following Scripture as an example: "My soul thirsts for God, the living God" (Ps. 42:3a).

An admiring and esteeming love—This fourth level of love begins to move the soul's desires from the sensory part to the spiritual part. This gift of love is given by God as a prelude to the next degree of love. At this stage, the soul esteems and admires God so greatly that it cannot bear the thought of offending God and losing Him. This is similar to the second degree of love, but now the "holy fear" is more spiritual in nature rather than in the sensory appetites. The soul feels as if God is not pleased with it, and as a result of the profound and mysterious admiration it has for God, it suffers greatly, wondering if God has left it. But in the midst of this suffering (which comes from fear of losing God), the soul still greatly esteems God. This person may need the assurance that not all is lost, that God is closer than ever, even though the soul feels Him not. Although this experience is painful, the soul begins to love God in an even purer way and is prepared to enter into the final degree of purgation of love.

Enkindling with an impassioned love in the spirit—
As the soul is infused with the spiritual blessings of God's love, it experiences both suffering and yearnings of love for God. The soul feels wounded and pierced by God's love, and this hurts. But this wound also stirs up a strong <u>spiritual</u> longing for love. Thus, despite the suffering, the soul longs for more. The desire is not on the level of one's senses and affections, it is a spiritual longing.

The soul endures affliction as it experiences yearnings. It suffers first by spiritual darkness in that it cannot see the remedy for its longings. But the soul also suffers from God directly, since God's presence draws it, even though it cannot see God nor find satisfaction in Him. Nonetheless, the soul seeks and searches for God, even though it feels alone, empty and weak. The soul believes itself to be miserable and unworthy of all love of God. However, even though the intellect perceives this, the <u>will</u> is infused with a fervent passion for God that is so strong that it is driven to seek God in everything. It may even act foolishly, with a blinding love, because the passion of love is so strong. This is not a willed love, but a spiritually infused passion in the will driving the person.

In reality, the soul is growing closer and closer to God. But the experience is one of darkness since its soul is finite and unable to receive the fullness of God. Thus, by receiving God in this infused way, the soul is overwhelmed and must be transformed, so that it can receive this pure infusion of divine love. This is like trying to pour the entire ocean into a small bottle. This can be done only by the hand of God.

Nonetheless, even though the mind cannot understand the fullness of God, the will is enkindled with the love of God it receives. Thus, it loves in darkness and blindness and begins to be enkindled with yearnings to love God more. Though this is a pure spiritual longing, the senses join in and follow. Nonetheless, the longing is first and foremost a spiritual passion. The soul burns with an unsatiated thirst for God. This passion is consented to by the will but is infused by God. It longs for the Beloved that it cannot find. Saint John also points to this Scripture as an illustration: "O God, you are my God—it is you I seek! For you my body yearns; for you my soul thirsts, in a land parched, lifeless, and without water" (Psalm 63:2).

Mary Magdalene had this love when she went to the tomb to find Jesus. When she realized Jesus was no longer in the tomb, her only desire was to find Him. She burned with a longing for her Lord and was undeterred in her search for Jesus. Saint John explains that she paid no attention to the angels in the tomb because she was so fixated on finding Jesus.

Final Journey into the Darkness of Virtue

For most people, the idea that one's senses and spirit must become "darkened" is new. Remember that Saint John is writing of the highest heights of perfection, which is something few people have experienced in this life. So if the language and descriptions of this "dark night" seem obscure and confusing, know that your experience is normal. Learning these lessons will be like learning an entirely new language and culture. The ideal way to do this is to forget everything that you knew before. It will be necessary that you begin to think in a new way, trying to understand God and your own life through an unfamiliar language imparted by God Himself.

Below are some of the benefits the soul will receive as it journeys through the darkness of this final purgation and annihilation of its former self, discovering a new life and a new unity with God. Saint John bases his teaching below on the following stanzas of his poem:

> In darkness and secure,
> By the secret ladder, disguised—oh, happy chance!—
> In darkness and in concealment,
> My house being now at rest.

Darkness—First, the "darkness" means that the soul's former ways of understanding, imagining, thinking, feeling, experiencing, enjoying, etc., come to an end. Its former understanding of God and life disappears. Its ability to reflect on and ponder the truths of God becomes impossible. Its former feelings of consolation and delight in God end. The soul is now in darkness to all former ways of thinking, feeling and experiencing life and God.

Recall the image of the person who wants to gaze upon the Sun for an hour so as to take in the beauty of the Sun. The natural eye cannot accomplish this. The Sun is too much. So it is with the natural faculties of the soul: intellect, will, memory, feelings, emotions, appetites. These natural faculties of the soul CANNOT understand, see, figure out, hold, know, feel or experience God by themselves. God is too much. But God wants to communicate Himself to every soul nonetheless. To accomplish this, He <u>suspends</u> all the natural operations of the soul and communicates to it in a new and <u>secret</u>

way. As a result, the natural faculties of the soul (mind, will, memory, appetites, feelings, etc.) are suspended and darkened until they become accustomed to the overwhelming presence of God. Until fully purified, they will not suffice to receive God in His pure form. God is now communicated more directly and in a way that does not rely upon the soul's natural abilities. Hence, the faculties are darkened.

Secure—The reason that this encounter is "secure" is that the soul no longer makes errors of judgment regarding the things of God, because it does not rely upon its natural abilities. For example, if you spent months trying to figure God out, you would never be able to do so, and in fact, your ultimate conclusion would be an error. Thus, if God removes your ability to "figure Him out," then you are safe in that you will not fall into the error. The same logic can be applied to every natural ability: imagining, willing, feeling, experiencing, desiring, etc. Nothing natural is capable of engaging God in His pure form. Thus, God darkens everything natural so as to communicate to you *in a new language!* The "new language" is infused faith, hope and charity. These virtues are directly communicated to your soul, now in the most secure way, so that you will come to *know* God, *hope* in God, and *love* God in a way you could never do by yourself. You begin to *securely* share in the divine life of God in God's way, by God's ability, and through God's power alone!

Secret—Saint John also says that this new way to communicating with God is "secret," it is "by the secret ladder..." Imagine that you went on vacation to the most beautiful place on Earth. You gazed upon the most majestic mountains, the tallest and most ferocious waterfalls, looked out over the vast valleys and encountered the most sublime creatures. You took pictures of all you saw, and then when you returned home, you showed these pictures to a friend. Your friend may have enjoyed the pictures and been impressed, but seeing the pictures of what you saw could never have imparted the same experience and knowledge of actually seeing those natural wonders in person.

Likewise, and to an infinitely greater degree, when God communicates to you His divine essence, by the gift of divine contemplation, no "picture" you try to take in your mind will ever suffice. The knowledge and experience you gain of God is beyond words, beyond concepts, beyond language, and even beyond your natural ability to comprehend. Thus, this communication of God to you is "secret" in that its full picture is hidden from your natural faculties. No human concept suffices to understand, let alone express, that which you encounter by infused faith. Therefore, this communication from God is of an entirely new form that you have never known before. It transcends all conceptual knowledge and is simply indescribable!

Ladder—Saint John describes ten steps of a mystical ladder, the *secret ladder*, of divine love. The ladder rests on the Beloved, God Himself, and the soul ascends and descends it as the soul presses on through this dark night of the spirit. At first the soul ascends, but as it fails in virtue, it then is humiliated and descends. The soul goes up and then down, experiencing humiliation and exaltation in its communication with God. Eventually, when perfected and purified, the soul arrives at the Beloved. Below are ten steps of a mystical ladder rising to divine love.

Step One—On this first step, the soul suffers agony because it is only on the first step. It feels sick with love and desires to be with God. Upon seeing how far away it is, the soul loses all delight in worldly things, and its suffering from want of God draws the soul upward.

Step Two—On this second step, the soul begins to seek God without ceasing. It walks with a sort of spiritual anxiety wanting nothing but its Beloved. All its words and thoughts are of God. God is the soul's only concern.

Step Three—On this third step, the soul experiences a new fervor to work without failure in its pursuit of the Beloved. It labors greatly and with eagerness. It takes on great works but sees them as small. The soul considers itself useless and living in vain, because, despite its fervor, it cannot do enough for God, and the little it does seems like nothing. All the soul's works are seen as imperfect, and this causes suffering. Vainglory disappears; the soul's only desire is the glory of God.

Step Four—On this fourth step, the soul does not become weary. Nothing hinders it in its pursuit of its Beloved. It only desires to please God. However, there is great suffering in the soul, but this suffering produces good, because the soul pays no attention to the suffering and seeks only to love and serve God. Perseverance through suffering makes the soul strong.

Step Five—On this fifth step, the soul begins to desire God impatiently. Every delay in reaching the Beloved is wearisome. In fact, the soul is so anxious to find its Beloved, that time and time again it thinks it has found Him, then realizes it hasn't. But every disappointment leaves the soul hungry for God, and this hunger becomes a nourishment to seek more.

Step Six—On this sixth step, the soul runs swiftly and begins to discover the Beloved. It is filled with hope and never wearies. Again and again, it reaches out and touches the Beloved, only to lose hold of Him. But every touch fires the soul with more hope and fervor.

Step Seven—On this seventh step, the soul becomes very bold. Though it is aware of its grave imperfections, it boldly lunges forward to its Beloved. Neither shame nor counsel nor anything deters it from boldly pursuing God. The boldness is on account of love. As St. Paul says, "[Love] bears all things, believes all things, hopes all things, endures all things. Love never fails" (1 Corinthians 13:7-8b).

Step Eight—On this eighth step, the soul seizes the Beloved and does not let go. The soul is finally satisfied, but it does not last because the Beloved slips away, and the soul falls down to a lower step on the ladder again.

Step Nine—Finally, the soul arrives at perfection! On this ninth step, the soul unites with its Beloved and it burns with the incredible sweetness of God. The Holy Spirit causes this burning sweetness. The best explanation Saint John gives of this step is to say that we cannot even explain it. There is no way to describe this encounter with the Beloved.

Step Ten—This final step is not for this world. Though some souls may make it to this step in this life, they do so only by leaving the body and becoming fully assimilated to God. If this happens in this life, it occurs only for brief moments. These souls are purified to the perfect degree, and if they died would immediately see the Beatific vision.

Disguised—The final benefit of the dark night of the spirit is that the soul climbs the ladder to God "disguised." Saint John explains that the disguise conceals the soul from the three enemies: devil, world and flesh.

Faith, the white garment covering the soul, voids the understanding of all its natural intellectual power so that it can know only on the divinely infused level of pure faith. The "disguise" of faith hides the intellect from the devil so that the devil has no way to trick or mislead the soul, since it is covered. It no longer understands by its natural abilities, which are imperfect, but understands only by the mind of God. Thus, the soul is prepared, by this new understanding, for union with God.

Hope, the green garment, covers the white garment and represents the infused gift of supernatural hope. Hope empties the memory of all worldly things, thus protecting it from the enemy the world. The soul no longer is drawn to anything the world can offer it and has no interest in anything except the one object of hope that is infused into its memory: hope in God and hope for union with God alone. Thus, by hoping in nothing but God, the soul is prepared for union with God.

Charity, the purple garment, covers the white and green garment and voids the will of every love other than God and His holy will. Charity protects the soul from the enemy the flesh, because all the selfish loves the flesh tempts it with are of no interest. The flesh cannot take hold of the will, since it is covered by this garment of charity, which is love of God alone.

Therefore, now fully disguised and hidden from the devil, the world and the flesh, the soul is free to pursue one thing: God. God fills its understanding, its memory and its will. God alone covers, protects and directs the soul to union with Him.

A sheer grace—Saint John explains that he spent many pages describing the painful purgations so that the soul would come to realize what a grace it is to walk through them and attain divine union. It is easy for people to become discouraged along the way by the suffering they endure. Therefore, if they know that these purgations lead to union, they will have more hope during the long journey to this "sheer grace!"

The Final Purgation of the Final Night

Saint John concludes his exposition on the "Dark Night of the Spirit" by explaining that the soul must press on through the deepest darkness, seeking God alone so as to be at rest and to be properly prepared for the divine union that awaits. This *final purgation* of the *final dark night* is a state of spiritual betrothal and is accomplished only by the most secret contemplation of God in the depths of the spirit without the lights of anything within the lower part of the soul (the senses) nor anything in the higher part of the soul (the intellect, memory and will). No feeling, concept, memory, object of rational desire nor anything else except the pure, silent, hidden and mysterious communication of God Himself to the spirit suffices.

The devil will not be able to see this communication of secret contemplation from God, but he will be aware that something glorious is taking place, because he will see that the lower part of the soul is entering into complete rest. The devil may even be able to see, by God's permission, the work of good angels assisting the soul. As a result, the devil will be able to torment the soul in a spiritual way as one final trial. But God permits this trial during the period of betrothal only to purify the soul on the deepest level. In the end, if the soul seeks God and God alone, and silences <u>everything</u> in its senses AND all things in its intellect, memory and will, it will receive the purest communication of God in the most silent and hidden way, through pure contemplation, while all the faculties of the soul are in pure darkness. In this darkened contemplation, the soul receives God Himself and the devil, the world and the flesh are powerless to hinder it.

The soul in the state of betrothal is now fully prepared for the glory of divine union. The soul is completely at rest, receiving everything from God alone in the most secret depths of its being, as described by Saint John of the Cross's famous poem as follows:

A Third Conversion

<u>Dark Night of the Soul</u>

On a dark night,
Kindled in love with yearnings—oh, happy chance!—
I went forth without being observed,
My house being now at rest.

In darkness and secure,
By the secret ladder, disguised—oh, happy chance!—
In darkness and in concealment,
My house being now at rest.

In the happy night,
In secret, when none saw me,
Nor I beheld aught,
Without light or guide, save that which burned in my heart.

This light guided me
More surely than the light of noonday
To the place where he (well I knew who!) was awaiting me–
A place where none appeared.

Oh, night that guided me,
Oh, night more lovely than the dawn,
Oh, night that joined Beloved with lover,
Lover transformed in the Beloved!

Upon my flowery breast,
Kept wholly for himself alone,
There he stayed sleeping, and I caressed him,
And the fanning of the cedars made a breeze.

> The breeze blew from the turret
> As I parted his locks;
> With his gentle hand he wounded my neck
> And caused all my senses to be suspended.
>
> I remained, lost in oblivion;
> My face I reclined on the Beloved.
> All ceased and I abandoned myself,
> Leaving my cares forgotten among the lilies.

While Saint John completed his commentary on the first three stanzas of his poem *Dark Night of the Soul*, he either never finished his commentary on the last five stanzas or those writings were lost. However, the next chapter of this book will turn to the *Spiritual Canticle* and the *Living Flame of Love*, which are two other poems written and explained by Saint John that do cover the same content included in the final five stanzas of the *Dark Night of the Soul*.

Chapter Five

The Journey Was Worth It!

Betrothal and Spiritual Marriage

Betrothal is that final state just prior to the permanent union of God with the soul. It is the final part of the *passive purgation of the spirit*, a transitional stage from the Illuminative Way to the Unitive Way. In this state, the flesh, the world and the devil may still attack the soul and attempt to distract it and draw it out of the union it enjoys. Though the soul begins to enjoy the blessings of this union, it needs strength, courage and countless virtues to infuse it so that it can enter into the permanence of divine marriage. Once divine marriage is achieved, neither the devil, the flesh nor the world have any power over it whatsoever. It is perfectly at rest with the Beloved.

Saint John's close companion, Saint Teresa of Ávila, explains the difference between these two states by saying that betrothal is like two candles that are lit and touched together at the wick. Suddenly, the flame burns as one. The two are perfectly united. However, she also explains that this is not a permanent state in that it is possible for the candles to be separated again. Thus, betrothal brings union with God but not in the permanent way that marriage does. The soul is united to God, but the temptations of the flesh, the world and the devil still attack and seek to separate them from each other.

Spiritual marriage is like rain falling into a river. Once the drops enter the river, it is not possible to remove them. They are so mingled that, even though they remain distinct, they are forever united. The drops of rain become part of the mighty river.

In the *The Spiritual Canticle*, Saint John of the Cross explains the state of betrothal in Stanzas 14-21. This is a state wherein the soul moves from the painful purgations of its last imperfections to that of pure union. The union of betrothal is a spiritual union. However, the bodily senses are not yet fully united to God. Saint John explains it this way:

> But before I proceed to explain the stanzas which follow, I must observe that, in the state of betrothal, wherein the soul enjoys this tranquillity, and wherein it receives all that it can receive in this life, we are not to suppose its tranquillity to be perfect, but that the higher part of it is tranquil; for the sensual part, except in the state of spiritual marriage, never loses all its imperfect habits, and its powers are never wholly subdued, as I shall show hereafter. What the soul receives now is all that it can receive in the state of betrothal, for in that of the marriage the blessings are greater. Though the bride-soul has great joy in these visits of the Beloved in the state of betrothal, still it has to suffer from His absence, to endure trouble and afflictions in the lower part, and at the hands of the devil. But all this ceases in the state of spiritual marriage. (*The Spiritual Canticle* 15.10)

In this state of betrothal, the soul is united to God in the spirit. Though the lower part of the soul remains imperfect and the devil continues to try to inflict harm upon the soul, the spirit remains vigilant and at peace. This temporary state of betrothal, however, eventually gives way to the permanent state of marriage.

In marriage, every part of the soul, spiritual and sensual, is transformed by God and shines brightly with the light of the Holy Spirit. By analogy, it's like the stars in the sky on a sunny day. The stars are still there, shining brightly, but they are invisible because the brightness of the Sun overwhelms them. So it is with every faculty, desire and passion of the soul. The entire soul, spirit and senses, takes on the brightness of the Holy Spirit and radiates as if the soul were God and God were the soul. The two are united without either losing their identity. The union transforms; it does not destroy. All the lower loves of the soul, every other attachment it formerly had, and all former concepts and experiences are annihilated so that God and God alone takes possession of and lives in and through the soul. It is this last, unquenchable enkindling with an impassioned love of God that enables the soul to cling to and become one with its Beloved.

> When the soul has lived for some time as the bride of the Son, in perfect and sweet love, God calls it and leads it into His flourishing garden for the celebration of the spiritual marriage. Then the two natures are so united, what is divine is so communicated to what is human, that, without undergoing any essential change, each seems to be God—yet not perfectly so in this life, though still in a manner which can neither be described nor conceived. (*The Spiritual Canticle* 22.5b)

In this state of divine union, the soul realizes that every purgation it has endured was worth it. There will be no regrets, only gratitude beyond imagination that the soul persevered through the long journey to union. Saint John identifies two final blessings for the soul who has entered through the purgation of the senses and the purgation of the spirit. First, in this life the soul enjoys habitual union with God, as briefly described in the quote above. This is the life of earthly perfection. However, Saint John also points out that even more awaits the soul: the Beatific Vision. While on Earth, the soul will live in perfect union with God and experience the fullness of the life of God. But that fullness of life in God is elevated once the soul dies and enters into the glory of Heaven, beholding the face of God in the Beatific Vision.

The Living Flame of Love

The experience of divine union is beyond words. However, Saint John of the Cross attempted, nonetheless, to speak of this union using a poetic presentation. The poem describes the sweetness and the burning intimacy felt by the soul, having finally reached God the Beloved after such a dark and painful journey to be with Him.

Stanzas the Soul Recites in Intimate Union with God:

> O Living Flame of Love,
> That woundest tenderly
> My soul in its inmost depth!
> As thou art no longer grievous,

Perfect thy work, if it be thy will,
Break the web of this sweet encounter.

O sweet burn!
O delicious wound!
O tender hand! O gentle touch!
Savouring of everlasting life,
And paying the whole debt,
By slaying Thou hast changed death into life.

O lamps of fire,
In the splendours of which
The deep caverns of sense,
Dim and dark,
With unwonted brightness
Give light and warmth together to their Beloved!

How gently and how lovingly
Thou wakest in my bosom,
Where alone Thou secretly dwellest;
And in Thy sweet breathing
Full of grace and glory,
How tenderly Thou fillest me with Thy love.

Saint John assisted his readers by writing a commentary on each stanza to explain the deeper meaning behind this poem. This same structure will be used below as follows.

Stanza 1:

O Living Flame of Love,
That woundest tenderly
My soul in its inmost depth!
As thou art no longer grievous,
Perfect thy work, if it be thy will,
Break the web of this sweet encounter.

The "Living Flame" is the Holy Spirit. The soul cries out "O" as an expression of its deepest longings of love. The Holy Spirit has now fully enflamed the soul and the soul expresses its deepest love of God, desiring all the more to enter deeply into that love. The soul is "tenderly wounded" or "cauterized" by love. It may seem like a paradox to say that love wounds, but it does so only to heal, just as hot metal cauterizes a wound. Love has tenderly healed the soul by freeing it from everything not of God. Every touch of God draws the soul closer and brings greater healing, freedom and divine transformation. This experience of God's most tender love will continually deepen for all eternity.

Saint John once again recalls the image of the log that he described in *The Dark Night*. He explains that the soul being purified by God's love is like a burning log. As it crackles and burns, its impurities are released. The soul becomes humbled by the blackened soot that surrounds it. Yet slowly, the fire begins to transform the log just as God's love begins to transform the soul.

At this stage of spiritual development, the soul rejoices with exuberant exultation, because it is not only fully purified of all attachments, but also because its "inmost depth" has been set ablaze by the Holy Spirit. The soul and God are now one, united in the flame of God's perfect love. Nothing impure remains. Everything within the deepest center of the soul is changed and transformed. All is ablaze with the love of God, and the love of God radiates forth. God Himself becomes the center of the soul, and the soul rests in this inner center of the life of God Himself.

Recall that during the Purgative and Illuminative Way of the beginner and proficient, the soul was purified by the love of God. This "Living Flame" afflicted the disordered appetites and imperfect faculties. But now, the Living Flame, the Holy Spirit, no longer afflicts anything within the soul. The "fire" no longer purges since all is purged. It flickers with warmth and beauty because the Living Flame is one with the soul on every level. As a result, the soul begins to think with the mind of God, delights in the memories of God and loves with the will of God. Love's delight is so strong and glorious that the soul longs for Heaven.

Recall also that at various times, as the soul went through the purgations of sense and spirit, it longed for death. This longing was primarily a result of its painful purgations and also because it humbly saw much wretchedness within itself. However, now that all sin and all disorder are completely dispelled from the soul, it longs to die now out of love. It is now the Holy Spirit who enkindles a spiritual longing to "break the web" of this life and enter into the Beatific Vision of Heaven. First, God broke the soul free from the sensory attachments. Second, He broke the soul free from the spiritual imperfections within the intellect, memory and will. Now, the soul, being one with God, desires to have its spirit freed from the body so that the spirit can be with God in Heaven. The soul is consumed with love, and love directs the soul from the deepest center, flowing forth in joyful and exuberant abundance.

The poem continues with **Stanza 2**:

> O sweet burn!
> O delicious wound!

> O tender hand! O gentle touch!
> Savouring of everlasting life,
> And paying the whole debt,
> By slaying Thou hast changed death into life.

The second stanza treats the same subject but from a different perspective. These lines identify the unique workings of each person of the Blessed Trinity. The "sweet burn" and "delicious wound" come from the Holy Spirit. The "tender hand" is that of the Father. And the "gentle touch" is the touch of the Son.

The Holy Spirit—The "sweet burn" of the Holy Spirit accomplishes a cauterizing of the soul. Cauterizing is a form of healing by burning. However, this burning of the deepest center of the soul by the Holy Spirit does not cause any pain since all sin is already removed. As a result, the only effect the soul experiences from this burn is health, strength and the sweetest delight. The fire of the Holy Spirit is powerful. In fact, it is so powerful that it could consume "a thousand worlds." But in this case, the soul absorbs the Living Flame of love and glows with its brightness and beauty.

The touch of the Holy Spirit continually wounds the soul, but every touch heals the previous wound. Thus, touch after touch after touch wounds and heals and wounds and heals and so on. With every touch there is greater transformation and delight. This divine touch does not communicate images, concepts or forms. It is the pure Spirit of God touching the pure spirit of the soul, communicating with it in a way purely spiritual.

The Father—God is all-powerful. With His mighty hand, He controls Heaven and Earth. Saint John recalls the following Scripture passages that illustrate such power by the hand of the Father:

> Who looks at the earth and it trembles, touches the mountains and they smoke! (Psalm 104:32).
>
> It is I who bring both death and life, I who inflict wounds and heal them, and from my hand no one can deliver (Deuteronomy 32:39).

However, the Father is also tender with His hand. He is generous and bountiful, and He showers us with mercy and kindness. Ultimately, through the Father's gentle hand, He gave us His human touch of love and healing through the gift of His Son, Jesus Christ.

The Son—Therefore, the Son of God, sent from the Father, is the delicate touch that Saint John describes. The Son touches the soul in its inner substance. This touch has the effect of absorbing the soul completely into the divine essence. The touch of the Son is so gentle and yet so powerful that the soul can be touched by nothing else, nothing of this world nor of the devil nor of the flesh. The touch of the Son of God alone takes possession of the soul.

This touch of the Son not only produces the fullest delight in the spirit, but also overflows into the body and senses. Additionally, the soul is given many gifts such as fortitude, wisdom, love, beauty, grace, patient endurance and goodness.

The soul is now a new creation. The death of its former self has resulted in new life in God. In this new state, the intellect no longer relies upon the senses and human reasoning as the source of its knowledge, but now knows purely by the mind of God. The will is not drawn to any natural affection nor to anything other than God Himself. The will of God is now the sole motivation of the human will, since both wills now are united as one. And the memory no longer occupies itself with anything of this world but is fixed on eternity alone. Though the soul remains distinct from God, it can be said that it becomes divinized, becoming God by participation and union. The unity is so profound that every thought, desire, passion, will, memory, etc., is completely directed by God and is in His perfect possession.

The poem continues with **Stanza 3**:

> O lamps of fire,
> In the splendours of which
> The deep caverns of sense,
> Dim and dark,
> With unwonted brightness
> Give light and warmth together to their Beloved!

Imagine a dark room in which one bright lamp after another is lit. Imagine countless lamps filling one dark room. Each one of those lamps unites its light with the other to transform the darkness of the room (the deep cavern) into brightness. So it is in the soul. Each lamp is what we can call an attribute of God: Mercy, Wisdom, Omnipotence, Power, Beauty, and so on. God, in His very essence, IS His attributes. He is Mercy itself, Wisdom itself, Power itself, and so on.

When the soul enters into divine union, it participates in the very attributes of God. Wisdom, Mercy, Power, etc., flood the soul and shine so brightly within the soul, it is as if the soul possesses these attributes itself, and it does.

The attributes of God are like a blazing flame burning within the soul. Not only does the flame shine its light within the soul, but the flame also enkindles the very air within the soul. It transforms the air, making it into the flame. Thus, the soul becomes God by participation. This spiritual truth is beyond comprehension and explanation.

The "deep caverns" of the soul, namely, the depths of the intellect, memory and will, become so transformed in God that they shine the actual "light and warmth" of God back to God. The soul loves by the Power of the Beloved. It is loved by God and loves by God. It praises, worships and adores God by the transforming hand of God Himself.

The poem ends with Stanza 4:

> How gently and how lovingly
> Thou wakest in my bosom,
> Where alone Thou secretly dwellest;
> And in Thy sweet breathing
> Full of grace and glory,
> How tenderly Thou fillest me with Thy love.

This final stanza expresses the immense gratitude of the soul for two things. First, the soul thanks God for the gentle and loving "awakening" it experiences. Second, the soul is filled with gratitude at the "breathing" of God in the soul, which reveals the grace and glory of God and the heights to which the soul is drawn.

Awakening—The soul becomes aware of the "thousands upon thousands" of God's virtues and excellences. This awareness is beyond any conceptual knowledge. It's a pure spiritual knowledge given directly to the spirit by God Himself. The soul now sees all of creation through the mind of God Himself. All is understood from the divine perspective, taught by God Himself. Though this knowledge is beyond human capacity, the soul is not overwhelmed since God sustains it in this knowledge.

Breathing—As for this breathing of God into the soul, Saint John says that he does not want to speak of this since anything he says about it will fall short of the reality. Words simply could never even come close to the reality of what takes place by the breath of God within the soul.

The Spiritual Canticle

Let us conclude the teaching of Saint John of the Cross by quoting him directly. These quotes are from the commentary on the final stanza of his poem *The Spiritual Canticle*—Stanza 40.2 and 40.3. Saint John begins by offering five blessings the soul receives in divine union:

> The first is that the soul is detached from all things and a stranger to them. The second is that the devil is overcome and put to flight. The third is that the passions are subdued, and the natural desires mortified. The fourth and the fifth are that the sensual and lower nature of the soul is changed and purified, and so conformed to the spiritual, as not only not to hinder spiritual blessings, but is, on the contrary, prepared for them, for it is even a partaker already, according to its capacity, of those which have been bestowed upon it.
>
> "None saw it."

> That is, my soul is so detached, so denuded, so lonely, so estranged from all created things, in heaven and earth; it has become so recollected in Thee, that nothing whatever can come within sight of that most intimate joy which I have in Thee. That is, there is nothing whatever that can cause me pleasure with its sweetness, or disgust with its vileness; for my soul is so far removed from all such things, absorbed in such profound delight in Thee, that nothing can behold me.

Saint John concludes his commentary on this sublime poem by stating that the soul now is left with a longing for Heaven. Though it is part of the "Church militant," meaning the Church on Earth, it longs to be drawn to the "Church triumphant," meaning the Church in Heaven. Thus, as described below in Stanza 40.8, the soul now waits until God draws it into the glory of the Beatific Vision for all eternity!

> All these perfections and dispositions of the soul the bride sets forth before her Beloved, the Son of God, longing at the same time to be translated by Him out of the spiritual marriage, to which God has been pleased to advance her in the Church militant, to the glorious marriage of the Church triumphant. Whereunto may He bring of His mercy all those who call upon the most sweet name of Jesus, the Bridegroom of faithful souls, to Whom be all honour and glory, together with the Father and the Holy Ghost, IN SECULA SECULORUM. AMEN.

Chapter Six

Summary and Practical Advice

Now that you have read through this overview of the mystical theology of Saint John of the Cross, you may find yourself wondering two questions: 1) Where am I on this journey? 2) What practically do I need to do to advance further? Though a well-trained spiritual director is the best guide for assisting in this area, finding a spiritual director, let alone one who is well-versed in the theology of the spiritual life, may actually be difficult for most people. Therefore, this chapter will first offer a summary of each stage of spiritual development and then conclude with some basic practical advice for each stage as well.

Summary of One's Initial Conversion

When a person first encounters God and receives from Him an interior call to conversion, he must choose to say "Yes" or "No." This initial conversion begins in one of two ways: *infant conversion* or *adult conversion*. Though Saint John of the Cross does not cover this initial conversion in his writings, he does presume that this initial conversion has already taken place.

Infant conversion: When a child is baptized, sanctifying grace is infused into its soul and Original Sin is removed. Thus, this infant is capable of communion with God. As the child grows and matures on a rational level, he will be continually invited to choose God over sin. If the toddler, child, adolescent, preteen and teen continues to be open to the voice of God speaking as he matures, then he will begin to develop a relationship with God from the earliest stages of development. Even a two-year-old will begin to understand right from wrong and will begin to grasp, albeit on a simplified level, an understanding of God. As the child grows into adolescence and teenage years, and if all along the way he continues to choose God and grows in his relationship with God, then the initial conversion takes place. Some children, such as Saint Thérèse of Lisieux, had a very deep relationship with God as early as the age of four. Of course, even with Saint Thérèse, her life of holiness continually deepened until the final year of her life (age 24) when she was most certainly living in the depths of the spiritual marriage.

Adult conversion: For others, whether they are baptized as infants or as adults, a spiritual conversion may not occur until later in life. This may be especially apparent in the lives of those who have been living in a state of habitual mortal sin. In this case, if at some point in their lives they are open to a special grace of God, inviting them to turn from sin and toward Him, and they do in fact make that choice, God's grace will rush upon them and bring about their initial conversion, setting them in a state of grace. Of course, when this happens to someone who has lived many years of habitual mortal sin, there is much purgation that needs to happen in their soul until it is capable of full communion with God. But this first step of conversion is essential.

A person who goes through this initial conversion, either as an infant who slowly grows in faith as he matures, or as an adult who turns away from a life of sin, will begin to walk as a new creation and will begin to grow in a knowledge and love of God.

Summary of the Active Night of the Senses

Saint John of the Cross begins his writings with a focus on the "beginner." He writes about this stage of spiritual development in his work *Ascent of Mount Carmel—Book I*. The beginner is one who is already initially converted to God, remains free from mortal sin and engages in a regular life of prayer and virtue. Sadly, when we consider all the people throughout the world, it appears that there are actually very few "beginners" who are on this path to perfection. Many people are still in need of initial conversion.

The goal of this "night" (purgation) is first to free the person from every attachment to habitual sin in the appetites. The second is to free the person from every habitual imperfection. Third is to free the person from even the voluntary desire for sin and every disordered affection. The primary focus is on the sensual nature of the soul. Later purgations will focus on the spiritual nature of the soul. This painful purgation of the sensual human nature (the appetites, passions, desires) will be helped by prayer, mortification and intentional acts of virtue. The Sacraments of Penance and the Eucharist will also be of great value.

The *Seven Capital Sins* are a primary focus of this purgation. The sins will be dealt with in a direct way, helping the soul to eliminate venial sins, imperfections and desires for these sins, and even helping to be freed of the commission of future mortal sins.

Discursive Meditation is the prayer that this person will find most beneficial. This form of meditation includes actively reading and pondering the Gospels in a prayerful way, so as to allow God to speak to the soul and guide it through its senses, desires, inspirations and spiritual consolations.

Passionate love for God will be this person's experience. The soul will have a zeal for God, virtue and other spiritual practices. In Saint John's words, the soul will be "**Kindled in love with yearnings**."

Summary of the Passive Night of the Senses

Saint John explains this step of the spiritual journey in the *Dark Night of the Soul—Book I*. The person going through this stage of spiritual development is in a transitional phase between being a "beginner" and a "proficient."

In this night (purgation), the soul is purified primarily by an act of God, not by anything it can do on its own. Like Step One, this purgation focuses upon the sensory appetites and desires a person has, but in a deeper way. After the soul is freed from all inordinate attachments and desires in the first step, it will come to realize that it also has many deep spiritual sins.

Summary and Practical Advice

The Seven Capital Sins are looked at in detail during this purgation, but now in a deeper spiritual way. In this stage of spiritual development, the soul will come to realize, through ongoing inspirations from God, that it has so delighted in the things of God that it has many spiritual attachments to the sensory pleasures it has received from its life as a beginner. For example, a soul may be so impressed with its own spiritual journey and virtue that it is filled with spiritual pride. Or it may enjoy the feelings of being close to God so much that it loves the feelings more than God (i.e., spiritual gluttony).

Purgative Contemplation is the prayer proper to this stage of spiritual development. When this happens, the soul will no longer find any satisfaction in the many spiritual consolations it has received, will find only dryness and bitterness in its senses, and will be invited by God to turn away from the many spiritual consolations it received when it was in the beginning stage of the spiritual journey. The dryness and loss of consolation is to draw the person to love of God in a more pure and spiritual way. Purgative contemplation will be infused directly by God, and not through the person's own efforts. The person will find it necessary to simply sit in silence before God, allowing God to do the work. The only responsibility of the person in this prayer is to consent to what God is doing.

Choosing God for God's Sake must be the single goal at this stage. Not because the soul finds consolation in loving God, but because God is worthy of love.

Summary of the Active Night of the Spirit

Saint John explains this step of spiritual development in Book Two and Three of the *Ascent to Mount Carmel*. The soul, now freed from all sensory attachments, including the many consoling sensory delights it received during its journey as a beginner, begins to turn its attention to the spiritual part of its inner self so as to surrender its intellect, memory and will to God in the deepest way.

In this night, the beginner is now a "proficient" in the spiritual life and enjoys an often lengthy period of stability, contemplative prayer and zeal for God. The soul grows in virtue and holiness but begins to sense that God wants more for it. As a result, the soul begins to allow God to infuse within it the pure gifts of faith, hope and charity. It begins to consciously "let go" of all former ideas of God, preferences for the future, selfish convictions about God's will, and it begins to choose a new level of oneness with God. The intellect begins to have faith in a more general and obscure way, as if the person were staring at the Sun. The memory begins to be purified and "forgotten." And the will is left in a sort of limbo, waiting upon the moment by moment gentle guidance of God.

Infused contemplation begins to become the normal method of prayer for the proficient. During this prayer, God communicates in a way that is mysterious but transforming. The soul is regularly drawn to God in prayer, but this prayer is not conceptual or meditative. Instead, the soul becomes more and more certain of the glory of God, but its certitude is more general, and less focused on specific ideas of God. The person spends much less time thinking *about* God and more time thinking of God in a more simple and direct way. Instead of having many hopes for itself, the person slowly learns to turn to one object of hope—God alone.

Choosing to let go of all former knowledge of God and striving to embrace His will must be the focus in this stage. This is so that the soul will be prepared for the total transformation it is about to undergo in the next and final purgation.

Summary of the Passive Night of the Spirit

Saint John explains this stage of spiritual development in Book Two of *The Dark Night of the Soul*. The soul undergoes its final purgation by means of a total annihilation of its former way of knowing, hoping and willing.

This final stage is a passive purgation in that it is an action of God, requiring only the consent of the soul. The person enters into a sort of "spiritual cocoon" in which the intellect, memory and will are completely transformed. The intellect comes to know God in a new way. It is darkened and forgets its former and lower knowledge of God and comes to know Him more certainly, but in an obscure way, trading concepts and ideas of God for the pure and overwhelming light of infused faith. The will is slowly purged entirely and lets go of everything except the will of God. Though the soul experiences great humility, feels utterly impoverished and empty, it is closer to God than ever before. In this darkness, the soul finds security and safety from the three enemies—the world, the devil and the flesh. These enemies no longer hinder it in any way. In this inner solitude and hiddenness, the soul becomes very strong and deeply resolved in its love for God. It is transformed by a "holy fear" of never wanting to offend God and only wanting to love Him and serve His holy will. In this fortitude of spirit, after relentlessly searching for and finding God, the soul now makes God and His perfect will the one and only object of its desire.

Habitual contemplative prayer becomes the norm, meaning that the soul has completely abandoned all lower forms of prayer and begins to walk always with God, praying always, and never tiring of loving God. Once the soul climbs the ladder to its Beloved, it is prepared for Divine Union.

Summary of Divine Union

Saint John explains this experience of the perfect soul in his works *Spiritual Canticle* Stanzas 22-40 and *The Living Flame of Love*. In this state of perfection, the soul is so intimately united to God that it shares fully in the divine attributes of God. Its intellect thinks with pure faith in God, its memory understands all things by the pure hope in God, its will is motivated by the pure charity of God, and all of its appetites, affections, desires and passions are completely ordered in God. The soul knows, understands, loves, feels, interacts and communicates in God and by God. The soul even loves God by the power of God Himself.

The primary image Saint John uses to describe this state of perfection is the log that is one with the flame and burns at its deepest center with the flame of the Holy Spirit.

Practical Advice for One's Initial Conversion

The best way to assure yourself of this initial conversion is to carefully, humbly and honestly go through the examination of conscience presented below. Once complete, if you are aware of any serious sin, you must firmly resolve to turn away from that sin and go to Confession. If you do not do this, God is greatly hindered in His ability to draw you closer to Him and set you down the journey of deeper conversion.

Examination of Conscience—Seven Capital Sins

Pride—Pride is an untrue opinion of ourselves, an untrue idea of what we are not. Have I a superior attitude in thinking or speaking or acting? Am I snobbish? Have I offensive, haughty ways of acting or carrying myself? Do I hold myself above others? Do I demand recognition? Do I desire to be always first? Am I ready to accept advice? Am I in any sense a "bully"? Am I inclined to be "bossy"? Do I speak ill of others? Have I lied about others? Do I make known the faults of others? Do I seek to place the blame on others, excusing myself? Is there anyone to whom I refuse to speak? Is there anyone to whom I have not spoken for a long time? Am I prone to argue? Am I offensive in my arguments? Have I a superior "know-it-all attitude" in arguments? Am I self-conscious? Am I sensitive? Am I easily wounded?

Envy—Envy is a sadness that we feel on account of the good that happens to our neighbor. Do I feel sad at the prosperity of others? At their success in games? In athletics? Do I rejoice at the failures and misfortunes of others? Do I envy the riches of others?

Sloth—Sloth is a kind of cowardice and disgust, which makes us neglect and omit our duties rather than discipline ourselves. Have I an inordinate love of rest, neglecting my duties? Do I act lazily? Am I too fond of rest? Do I take lazy positions in answering prayers? Do I kneel in prayer in a lounging way? Do I delight in idle conversation? Do I fail to be fervent in the service of God?

Lust—Lust is the love of the pleasures that are contrary to purity. Have I desired or done impure things out of selfishness? Have I taken pleasure in entertaining impure thoughts or desires? Have I read impure material, listened to music with impure lyrics, or looked at impure images, whether in photos or on television or in movies or on the Internet? Have I aroused sexual desire in myself or another by impure kissing, embracing, or touching? Have I committed impure actions alone, i.e., masturbation? Do I dress immodestly or am I too concerned with the way I look? Do I use vulgar language or tell or listen to impure jokes or stories? Have I given in to desires of adultery even in my imagination? Have I acted with seductive charm or been flirtatious?

Greed—Greed is a disordered love of the goods of this world. Do I dispose of my money properly or selfishly? Do I discharge my duties in justice to my fellow man? Do I discharge my duties in justice to the Church? Do I see money only as a means to serving God and others or do I see it as an end in itself? Do I obsessively think about wealth?

Gluttony—Gluttony is a disordered love of eating and drinking. Do I eat to live or live to eat? Do I drink to excess? Do I get drunk? Do I misuse prescription drugs? Do I use illegal drugs? Have I allowed myself to become addicted to alcohol?

Anger—Anger is an emotion of the soul, which leads us violently to repel whatever hurts or displeases us. Am I prone to anger? Does practically any little thing arouse my temper? Am I what is generally termed "a sore-head"? Do I fail to repress the first signs of anger? Do I fail to get along well with everybody? Do I ponder over slights or injuries and even presume them? Do I think of means of revenge? Of "getting even"? Am I of an argumentative disposition? Have I a spirit of contradiction? Am I given to ridicule of persons, places, or things? Am I hard to get along with? Do I carry grudges, remain "on the outs" with anyone? Do I talk about the faults of others? Do I reveal the faults or defects of others? Do I reveal the faults of others from the wrong motive?

Practical Advice for the Active Night of the Senses

Examination of Conscience—The examination of conscience on the Seven Capital Sins in the previous section should be returned to on a regular basis by the beginner. The active purgation of the senses requires that you be freed of all of these sins in a habitual way. Though you will never permanently be free from every venial sin until you enter fully into the Beatific Vision of Heaven, you must seek to eliminate every ingrained habit of sin. Using this examination of conscience in an ongoing and thorough way, coupled with the Sacrament of Reconciliation, will be of great importance to you achieving this purgation. Do not cease to examine your conscience with this method until God has truly freed you from every habitual sin identified.

In addition to the examination of conscience on the Seven Capital Sins, it will be helpful to carefully reflect upon the virtues that bring complete freedom from those sins. Below is an examination of conscience that presents the Seven Capital Virtues. These virtues will bring a much deeper freedom from all sin.

Examination of Conscience—Seven Capital Virtues

Humility—Humility cures pride and is ultimately knowing and believing the truth of who you are. Humility enables you to see yourself as God sees you. You will not find offense in the criticism of others. You are at peace even when you are unnoticed, misunderstood and misjudged. You will not take your identity in the opinions of others. You will regularly speak well of others, see goodness in them, and speak the truth without allowing your sin or the sins of others to cloud your judgment. You will be able to take responsibility for your failings, sincerely apologize as needed and regularly seek to heal discord.

Kindness—Kindness cures envy and leads a person to have a genuine love of neighbor, offering them unprejudiced, compassionate and charitable concern. You will find joy in the success of others and rejoice when they are sincerely honored and loved.

Diligence—Diligence cures sloth and leads a person to great zeal for goodness and for the accomplishment of the works of God. Love of God and others will be far more important to you than your own selfish comfort. Negative conversations will be of no interest. You will find joy and energy in doing what is right and beneficial to others.

Chastity—Chastity cures lust and will enable you to begin living in purity of mind and body. Sel<u>fish</u>ness will give way to sel<u>fless</u>ness in regard to disordered sexual desires. Others will no longer be looked upon as objects of desire, but will be seen as children of God our Father. The sacred dignity of each person will be revered in the way that is deserving of a child of God. Great care will be taken not to tempt, mislead or draw inordinate attention to yourself or your own body. Passions will be more easily mastered and brought under the control of the pure love of God. Chastity will especially be lived within marriage so that authentic and pure love can be shared between spouses and selfish love can be eliminated. Simply put, lust steals another's dignity but chastity affirms the dignity of all.

Liberality—Liberality is the cure for greed in that it will enable you to order your desires for material wealth in such a way that all is used for the single purpose of the greater glory of God. Money, or the lack thereof, presents each person with a powerful test. When you have much wealth, joy will be found in the use of that wealth for the good of others and the fulfillment of God's will. When you have little wealth, joy will be found in complete trust in God's providence. Simply put, liberality frees a person from an inordinate attachment to material wealth and even from the desire for it.

Temperance—Temperance cures gluttony in that it will enable you to act with self-control in regard to your desires for food and drink. Excessive cravings for food and drink will be eliminated and will be enjoyed in the ordered way God created them to be enjoyed. Simply put, food and drink will not control you.

Meekness—Meekness cures anger and will enable you to endure that which attempts to inflict harm upon you with patience and love. You will not be controlled by injustice but will respond to it with forgiveness. The ability to reconcile and be at peace with all people will grow strong. Sincere compassion will be offered to those who act with malice. Obsessive brewing over one's wounds will be eliminated and joy in suffering will grow in proportion to the suffering endured. Others will not be seen as enemies but will be seen with dignity, even if they do not act in a dignified way. Simply put, the malice of others or injustices endured will have no power over you.

Study—Another great help for the beginner will be to feed your mind with the truth by studying the Gospel and especially the person of Jesus. Read books about the Catholic faith, learn the *Catechism*, read the lives of the saints and continually strive to grow in a greater understanding of all that God has revealed to us through His Church. This knowledge will be a great help to you as you make a daily decision to turn from sin and turn to God. Though this practice will be of great benefit to the beginner, it is necessary for those in every stage of spiritual development. Therefore, make sure you have a regular and faithful plan of ongoing learning.

Prayer—The prayer proper to this stage of spiritual development is *discursive meditation,* which is a very careful, intentional and extended pondering of the Gospel and other truths God has revealed. This form of meditation is best practiced when you set aside at least 20 minutes, and ideally an hour, for prayer. Read one passage of the Gospel slowly. Reflect upon it and let God speak to you through it. After you feel you have fully pondered one passage, move on to the next, but not in a hurried way. This is not just reading of Scripture, it is meditating on it.

Sometimes meditation will be fueled by reflecting on beautiful prayers, especially those written by the saints. Therefore, find a good prayer book with traditional Catholic prayers and use those prayers for meditation. Meditating on prayers is not the same as simply saying or reading prayers. To meditate on them you must take time with them, make them personal, understand them, and mean every word.

Many people will find that daily devotionals, novenas, the rosary, chaplets, Stations of the Cross and various other forms of prayer will assist them in their meditations. Try new methods, new devotionals, reflections and inspirational meditations. When one feeds your prayer and draws you closer to God, stick with it.

Savor Spiritual Consolations—Sometimes, in prayer or study, God speaks to you in a powerful way. This is a grace, a sensible consolation sent from God to emphasize some particular truth that He wants you to focus on. Therefore, if something strikes you in the Scripture or your spiritual reading, make sure to "chew" on it, ponder it over and over and soak up all that God wants to communicate to you through this inspiration. At this stage of spiritual development, spiritual consolations and inspirations are quite common and useful, so be grateful for them when they come. In the next stage of spiritual development, this form of communication from God to you will end, so that God can communicate to you on an even deeper level. But as long as the consolations and inspirations come to you, receive them and let them help you to change.

Spiritual Maxims—Saint John offers us various spiritual maxims for meditation and prayer. These maxims will be challenging to read and even more challenging to desire. But remember, they come to us from perhaps the greatest spiritual doctor of the Church. You can trust that if these maxims are hard to embrace and live, that is because you need to be changed, not because there is

Summary and Practical Advice

something wrong with the maxim itself. Therefore, if you want to walk through this stage of the active night of the senses, try to spend time reflecting upon these maxims and live them to the best of your ability.

These maxims call the soul to strive to always <u>prefer</u> the *most difficult* rather than the *easiest*, the *least pleasant* rather than the *most pleasant*, the *most wearisome* rather than the most *restful*, and so on. When they are pondered, they will have the effect of revealing to you all selfishness. You may react negatively at first, but this is an intellectual exercise by which you can bring to the surface the various weaknesses, sins, selfish tendencies and the like, so that they can be dealt with.

Therefore, meditate on these maxims and then ponder what comes to mind as you do. You may gain many very helpful insights that will enable you to become a much more selfless person. Use these maxims in an intellectual and moral exercise by which you will see your sinful tendencies in a more honest and humble way.

The maxims are as follows:

Strive always to <u>prefer</u>:

> Not that which is easiest, but that which is most difficult;
> Not that which is most delectable, but that which is most unpleasing;
> Not that which gives most pleasure, but rather that which gives least;
> Not that which is restful, but that which is wearisome;
> Not that which is consolation, but rather that which is disconsolateness;

> Not that which is greatest, but that which is least;
> Not that which is loftiest and most precious, but that which is lowest and most despised;
> Not that which is a desire for anything [to desire anything], but that which is a desire for nothing;
> Strive to go about seeking not the best of temporal things, but the worst.
> Strive thus to desire to enter into complete detachment and emptiness and poverty, with respect to everything that is in the world, for Christ's sake.

As mentioned, these maxims can, at first, seem contrary to happiness. But if they are practiced and lived, you will discover that they are the path to great delight and consolation. The soul will at first find them repugnant. Ignore that and seek to desire them anyway. The result will be a much better knowledge of who you are, and a clearer revelation of your selfish tendencies that need to be purged.

Once you have spent time on the above maxims (ideally weeks or months), continue to reflect on the ones that follow in the same way. They will also be hard to accept. But remember, they are not literal "commandments" from God; rather, they are exercises by which you will bring your selfishness and sins to the surface.

Further counsel to overcome: 1) concupiscence of the flesh, 2) concupiscence of the eyes, and 3) pride of life:

> First, let the soul strive to work in its own despite, and desire all to do so.
> Secondly, let it strive to speak in its own despite and desire all to do so.

> Third, let it strive to think humbly of itself, in its own despite, and desire all to do so.

With these reflections below, it's important to note, especially, the first part of each. "In order to arrive at having pleasure in <u>everything</u>..." Like the exercises above, these reflections will help free you from the lower pleasures, possessions, knowledge, etc., that many embrace with passion. God wants so much more for you. Therefore, use them as a way of letting God begin to bestow <u>everything</u> good upon you. The highest good that only God can give!

Obtaining true freedom flowing from humility:

> In order to arrive at having pleasure in everything, desire to have pleasure in nothing.
> In order to arrive at possessing everything, desire to possess nothing.
> In order to arrive at being everything, desire to be nothing.
> In order to arrive at knowing everything, desire to know nothing.
>
> In order to arrive at that wherein thou hast no pleasure, thou must go by a way wherein thou hast no pleasure.
> In order to arrive at that which thou knowest not, thou must go by a way that thou knowest not.
> In order to arrive at that which thou possessest not, thou must go by a way that thou possessest not.
> In order to arrive at that which thou art not, thou must go through that which thou art not.

> When thy mind dwells upon anything, thou art ceasing to cast thyself upon the All.
> For, in order to pass from the all to the All, Thou hast to deny thyself wholly in all.
> And, when thou comest to possess it wholly, Thou must possess it without desiring anything.
> For, if thou wilt have anything in having all, Thou hast not thy treasure purely in God.

If you found those painful then you are on the right track. Don't abandon the reflections above until you begin to remember them, think about them and understand the true wisdom in each one of them. They are very valuable exercises for you on your way to holiness.

Practical Advice for the Passive Night of the Senses

If you have successfully spent time with the meditations, maxims and other spiritual exercises spoken of in the previous section "Practical Advice for the Active Night of the Senses," and if you have established a strong life of prayer, probably over a number of years, then there will be a time when God begins to draw you deeper. That "deeper" will be <u>infused contemplation</u>.

In this stage, the soul begins to be purged by God Himself rather than through its own efforts of mortification and self-denial. Two suggestions will be offered here for those whose senses are passively being purified by God through the invitation to infused contemplation.

Summary and Practical Advice

Seven Capital Sins on a Spiritual Level—Return to Chapter Two and spend time in a holy hour meditating on the Seven Capital Sins as they are manifested in a new spiritual way. Once you are aware of how these spiritual sins affect you, it's time to let God do His purifying work. This purgation can only take place through the prayer of purgative contemplation. God will remove the cause of the sin by drying up your spiritual consolations and, in fact, many other spiritual delights you have enjoyed within your sensory appetites.

What do you do in this process of contemplative purgation? As God begins to work on you, drawing you into this contemplation of sensory purgation, consciously allow yourself to be changed. God will do the work, but you must not interfere. You will feel different, see things differently, feel a loss of spiritual delight, and not sense the presence of God in the same way as you used to.

Four Natural Passions of the Soul—Another area to be aware of is what Saint John identifies as the natural passions of joy, hope, sorrow and fear. Each one of these passions, when they are disordered, has the potential to lead you far away from God and His will. They will even leave you confused, thinking that you are serving God when you are, in reality, only reacting to a powerful and inordinate passion.

A good spiritual practice is to spend time examining how these four natural passions influence your life. For example, spend time with fear. What is it that you are fearful of? Does it control you? Do you base decisions on fear? If you do spend time looking deep at your motivations in life and find fear to be one of those motivations, then know that God wants to heal you and free you of the heavy burden that fear imposes. The same is true with the other natural passions. Be sure to understand each one well, not confusing them with spiritual joy, hope, sorrow or fear. All four of these can be gifts from God. We are NOT speaking of those passions. We are speaking of the disordered and misguiding natural passions that control you. Joy in things other than God and His will. Hope for things not in the will of God. Sorrow that results from selfishness. And fear that results from a lack of trust and surrender.

Contemplation, when it is from God and is infused into your soul, will have the effect of purifying you and freeing you from these natural passions when they go astray.

Practical Advice for the Active Night of the Spirit

Those who have been living a stable Christian life and have spent much time (often years) practicing meditation and works of charity, and who have learned much about God and the faith that He has revealed, will eventually find that their long and stable life of union with God will begin to change. Up until this point, the moments of contemplation they have received from God have had the effect of purifying them of their worldly delights as well as the spiritual delights they have received from their Christian living. They have endured dryness in their sensory appetites for worldly things and even for spiritual experiences. But they have persevered through that dryness, and their relationship with God has become more stable and less reliant upon spiritual consolations.

Summary and Practical Advice

Now, God wants to use contemplative prayer to purify the soul on an even deeper level. The intellect, memory and will must now be purified of former knowledge *about* God. Former hopes and ideas pertaining to God will begin to change. Charity will begin to be infused in a new way, leading the soul to serve God in a more direct way rather than by using one's own ideas and constructed hopes of what God may want. Below is a Scripture passage used in Chapter Three which will be good to reflect upon and understand. God wants to take you to a new level of knowing, hoping and loving.

> For we know partially and we prophesy partially, but when the perfect comes, the partial will pass away. When I was a child, I used to talk as a child, think as a child, reason as a child; when I became a man, I put aside childish things. At present we see indistinctly, as in a mirror, but then face to face. At present I know partially; then I shall know fully, as I am fully known. (1 Corinthians 13:9-12)

Below are three specific ways that were mentioned in Chapter Three on how to intentionally go about this change in knowing, hoping and loving:

1. **Knowing**—Seek to plunge your mind into the obscurity and blindness of pure faith. A good image for this would be to see God, with your mind's eye, as pure light, brighter than the Sun itself, shining down upon you. The brightness is so overwhelming that it blinds you of all other knowledge you have *about* God. His brightness is all you see in a general, obscure but certain way.

2. **Hoping**—Seek to forget all your memories about God. You will be tempted, time and time again, to think about God and your past relationship with Him rather than to just pray. You will be tempted to go through various reasoning processes, trying to put together various pieces of your life so as to arrive at what you think must be God. Forget it. Let it all go. Seek to have an empty memory so that God can fully possess your memory alone with His pure self. Your hope must be in God and for that which you do not see, understand or possess. It's a blind but certain hope infused by God.

3. **Loving**—Seek to let go of every choice you need to make. Detach from every preference, every spiritual desire, everything you "want" to do for God. Instead, simply rest in His will. Wait on Him. When He is ready, He will guide you at the right time in the right way. Only if you strip your will of all decisions and preferences can God fully possess your will with His. And only then will God's love be able to become the source of your daily choices. No longer do you choose based on your self-conceived desires. Rather, you choose and act because the Holy Spirit is inspiring you to act.

Simply put, the best practical advice for those engaged in the *active night of the spirit* is to understand that it is time to begin a transformation of the way you think, hope and act. God wants to draw you into adulthood and bring about a complete transformation within your spirit (intellect, memory and will). Your disordered affections and other habitual attachments have been quieted, but now you must look deeper. God wants to "reprogram" the deepest part of you. In order for that to happen, you must willingly allow yourself to be drawn into a process of "unknowing" so that you can come to know, hope and love in a way directly infused by God. For your part, <u>understand</u> what is happening and <u>consent</u> to the changes God wants to make in you.

Practical Advice for the Passive Night of the Spirit

As you actively seek to let go of your former ways of knowing, hoping and loving, and seek to discover the new and infused way God wants to bestow these three virtues upon you, you must ultimately surrender all and *accept* that which God wants to do within your soul. Though this stage is a *passive* stage, meaning it is something that God does in you far more than something you intentionally do, it will require that you continue the two main things mentioned above: 1) understanding, and 2) consent.

In order to understand and consent to that which God is doing, make sure you understand the following experiences you may have. Accept them when you experience them and renew your love and commitment to God in the midst of these experiences:

1. Allow yourself to see your sin, in all its misery, as God infuses you with new faith. Don't be overwhelmed but do acknowledge your wretchedness and weakness with honesty. This humbling realization should also be experienced as you see the infinite mercy of God. The truth of God's mercy will allow you to gaze more deeply

than you ever have before on your weakness and sin.
2. Think about Job, the good and faithful man, who was allowed to go through the most severe trial imaginable. He lost everything—his riches, family and even his physical health. His response was to sit in silence before the mystery of his wretchedness, while at the same time he renewed his hope and trust in God. He didn't complain, explain away his misery, or lose hope. He simply acknowledged the greatness of God in His lowly state. Reading through the story of Job would be a great help in this stage of development.
3. Don't be afraid to allow your former self to die. You must be at peace as you remain still in this "cocoon" of God's transforming power. Accept that you are being changed by God and willingly consent to the transformation that God wants to bring about in you.
4. In this state, God will appear to be absent and silent. As a result, you will not be able to pray as you used to pray. Your prayer must become deeper and more intentional as you experience the apparent loss of God's presence. Recall Psalm 22, which was perfectly prayed by Jesus on the Cross as an expression of both His interior experience of loss as well as His perfect trust in the Father. God will draw you to live that psalm also. It would be helpful to read the entire psalm over and over: "My God, my God, why have you abandoned me? Why so far from my call for help, from my cries of anguish? My God, I call by day, but you do not answer; by night, but I have no relief. Yet you are

> enthroned as the Holy One; you are the glory of Israel…" (Psalm 22:2-4).

Again, this stage of spiritual development is "passive," meaning, God will do the work in you. You must make sure you do not hinder what He wants to do in you, and the best way to do this is to make sure that these four points above are understood and embraced.

It's also important to point out that you cannot force this passive purgation of your spirit to happen. There is nothing you can do to initiate it other than to wait on God's purifying action. Therefore, if you find you are not sure what to do at this point, then do nothing. Wait on the Lord and work on the former spiritual practices. When the time comes for God to draw you into this spiritual purgation, understanding the four points above will help prepare you for it.

Practical Advice is Not Needed for Those in Divine Union

The final step of the spiritual journey is that of the perfect. Of this state, nothing can be said regarding practical advice. The soul who is living in this state of perfection will know all it needs to know directly from God Himself. God will fill this soul with every knowledge, understanding, love and hope contained within God Himself. However, here are a few final thoughts for your spiritual journey before reaching Transforming Union:

Don't rush it, but do rush it—On one hand, those who want to become holy will be tempted to rush it. They will want to enter into the state of perfection immediately and may become deluded into thinking that they are already close. Don't be that person. Humility must be so central in your life that you will not fall into the errors of spiritual pride, thinking and acting as if you are further along in your journey than you are. Therefore, regularly remind yourself that, in a real way, it doesn't matter how far along you are. What matters is that you daily seek to make progress. That's it. Make progress every day. If you slip and fall, get back up immediately and resume your journey. As long as you seek to make progress every day, you will be on the right path.

However, though spiritual pride could lead a person to think they are further along the journey than they are, spiritual sloth may lead them to think there is no rush. But there is a rush! There is no reason that every person reading this book should not seek to obtain the divine union of the perfect as soon as possible. Do not put it off until tomorrow; set your feet to the road and walk it vigorously today. Most importantly, let God lead. If you do, you will be eternally grateful.

Embrace the moment—Every stage of spiritual development brings with it its own incredible blessings. Savor each moment. Even the most painful purgations will eventually become sweet to you if you embrace them as God calls you to embrace them. As mentioned above, don't rush the path to holiness (meaning, don't try to move faster than God), because to do so would be a result of pride. But another reason not to falsely rush it and pretend you are further along than you are is because doing so will keep you from loving and savoring every moment of interior conversion you are given. The blessings along the way are glorious. Enjoy the journey as you keep your eyes fixed upon God who is your final goal.

***Keep your eyes fixed on the goal*—**Though every moment of the journey is glorious and full of rewards and spiritual treasures, the end is the goal. Therefore, as you enjoy the process of ongoing conversion, never take your eyes off the ultimate end: God Himself. Spiritual fulfillment, delights, virtues, experiences, consolations, etc., are not the ultimate end. God and God alone is the ultimate end. If you remember that, you will keep moving and keep seeing God in His fullness.

***The ultimate summary of Saint John of the Cross*—**Simply put, Saint John of the Cross reveals to us that everything in life is an obstacle to divine union unless it is completely transformed in Christ. Every attachment to sin, to the things of this world, disordered attachment to people, attachments to spiritual pleasure and every other attachment to anything other than to God alone is ultimately an obstacle to divine union. This is radical. But it's also true.

As you slowly come to understand the countless attachments you have in life, and as you begin to allow God to remove these attachments, you will begin to see that your love of God overflows in your life, leading you to love all things in Him, by Him and through Him. Your love of others, and even your love of the good things of this world, will flow from a new purified love residing in the Heart of God Himself. God's Heart, living in your heart, will be the instrument through which your life is ordered and experienced. Nothing could ever be better than this.

Scripture as a Basis for Saint John's Teaching

Below are a few of the Scripture passages Saint John uses as the basis of his teachings. These Scriptures come from Book I of the *Ascent* and primarily explain the active purgation of the senses. Though Saint John used many other Scriptures throughout his writings, the ones that follow help to illustrate the way Saint John based his teachings upon the Word of God. Prayerfully read them and let God speak to you through them so as to convince yourself of the necessity of these purgations.

Luke 14:33—"In the same way, every one of you who does not renounce all his possessions cannot be my disciple."

Exodus 34:1-3—Moses is called up the mountain alone. Saint John says this is to be seen as an image of every one of us being called up the mountain of perfection. We go up alone, without any attachments or desires. Furthermore, not even the beasts could graze in front of the mountain. This indicates that the appetites must not even be near us and cannot continue to occupy our attention, curiosity or desire. Thus, we ascend to God with nothing, detached from all.

Genesis 35:2—Jacob was called up the mountain and ordered the people to do three things: 1) Destroy all strange gods (This is an image of our interior affections and attachments). 2) Purify themselves (We must also be purified of the residue of the attachments we have renounced). 3) Change their garments (Our souls will have the old understanding removed, and a new understanding of God, in God, will take its place. All the former loves of the soul will be replaced by divine love. Thus, all human activities of the soul end and only divine activities remain).

Exodus 27:8—The altar for the Ark was to be empty and hollow so as to remind the soul that nothing foreign can mingle with worship of God.

Leviticus 10:1-2—Aaron's sons, Nadab and Abihu offered unauthorized fire to God. As a result, God struck them dead. This shows that we cannot offer fitting worship to God if we have "unauthorized" attachments in our soul. We cannot love God if our soul is mixed with alien loves.

1 Samuel 5:2-4—The Ark of the Covenant was placed in the temple next to an idol. The idol was subsequently thrown to the ground and broken by God. The manna, the Law and the rod of Moses are the only things that can be present in the Ark. The Manna represents God Himself (especially encountered in the Sacraments and prayer), the Law is God's Word (especially the Scripture) and the Rod of Moses is an image of the Cross (the only means of our transformation in Christ). If we want to be true arks of God, we must only possess the Law and the Cross. Then we will carry the true Manna within our souls (which is God).

Quotes of Saint John for Reflection

"Now that I no longer desire all, I have it all without desire." (from the "Sketch of Mount Carmel")

"So that, in order to come to union with the wisdom of God, the soul has to proceed rather by unknowing than by knowing." (*Ascent* 1.4.5)

"It is clear that the desires weary and fatigue the soul; for they are like restless and discontented children, who are ever demanding this or that from their mother, and are never contented. And even as one that digs because he covets a treasure is wearied and fatigued, even so is the soul wearied and fatigued in order to attain that which its desires demand of it; and although in the end it may attain it, it is still weary, because it is never satisfied." (*Ascent* 1.6.6)

"The soul is wearied and fatigued by all its desires and by indulgence in them, since they all cause it greater emptiness and hunger; for, as is often said, desire is like the fire, which increases as wood is thrown upon it, and which, when it has consumed the wood, must needs die." (*Ascent* 1.6.6)

"Even as vapours darken the air and allow not the bright sun to shine; or as a mirror that is clouded over cannot receive within itself a clear image; or as water defiled by mud reflects not the visage of one that looks therein; even so the soul that is clouded by the desires is darkened in the understanding and allows neither the sun of natural reason nor that of the supernatural Wisdom of God to shine upon it and illumine it clearly." (*Ascent* 1.8.1)

"If a man is to enter this Divine union, all that lives in his soul must die, both little and much, small and great, and that the soul must be without desire for all this, and detached from it, even as though it existed not for the soul, neither the soul for it." (*Ascent* 1.11.8)

Summary and Practical Advice

"To reach satisfaction in all, desire satisfaction in nothing. To come to possess all, desire the possession of nothing. To arrive at being all, desire to be nothing. To come to the knowledge of all, desire the knowledge of nothing. To come to enjoy what you have not, you must go by a way in which you enjoy not. To come to the possession you have not, you must go by a way in which you possess not. To come to what you are not, you must go by a way in which you are not." (*Ascent* 1.13.11)

"When thy mind dwells upon anything, thou art ceasing to cast thyself upon the All." (*Ascent* 1.13.12)

"It is clear, then, that faith is dark night for the soul, and it is in this way that it gives it light; and the more the soul is darkened, the greater is the light that comes to it. For it is by blinding that it gives light." (*Ascent* 2.3.4)

"A soul may lean upon any knowledge of its own, or any feeling or experience of God, yet, however great this may be, it is very little and far different from what God is; and, in going along this road, a soul is easily led astray, or brought to a standstill, because it will not remain in faith like one that is blind, and faith is its true guide." (*Ascent* 2.4.3)

"For, in telling us to look to the faith whereof the prophets spake, as to a candle that shines in a dark place, he is bidding us remain in the darkness, with our eyes closed to all these other lights; and telling us that in this darkness, faith alone, which likewise is dark, will be the light to which we shall cling; for if we desire to cling to these other bright lights -- namely, to distinct objects of the understanding -- we cease to cling to that dark light, which is faith, and we no longer have that light in the dark place whereof Saint Peter speaks." (*Ascent* 2.16.15)

"Some beginners, too, make light of their faults, and at other times indulge in immoderate grief when they commit them. They thought themselves already saints, and so they become angry and impatient with themselves, which is another great imperfection. They also importune God to deliver them from their faults and imperfections, but it is for the comfort of living in peace, unmolested by them, and not for God; they do not consider that, were He to deliver them, they would become, perhaps, prouder than ever. They are great enemies of other men's praise, but great lovers of their own, and sometimes they seek it. In this respect they resemble the foolish virgins, who, when their lamps gave no light, went about in search of oil, saying: 'Give us of your oil, for our lamps are going out.'" (*Dark Night* 1.2.5)

"The more [the soul] is purified and cleansed in the fire of love, the more it glows with it. The better the fuel is prepared for the fire the better it burns. The soul, however, is not always conscious of this burning of love within it, but only now and then, when the contemplation is less profound, for the soul is then able to observe, and even to delight in, the work that is being wrought, because it is visible; the hand of the artificer seems to be withdrawn from the work, and the iron taken out of the furnace, so as to show in some measure the work that is being wrought. Then, too, the soul is able to see in itself that good which it did not see while the process was going on. Thus, when the flame ceases to envelop the fuel, it is possible to see clearly how much of it has been burnt." (*Dark Night* 2.10.7)

"[The soul] sallied forth unknown to the whole of its household by a most secret ladder, which, as I shall show in the proper place, is a living faith—in such secrecy and silence, for the better execution of its purpose, that it could not possibly be in greater security; especially now, because in the purgative night, the desires, passions, and affections of the soul are asleep, mortified, and subdued; and these are they which, awake and active, would never have consented to that departure." (*Dark Night* 2.15.2)

"But, to speak with more accuracy, and to the purpose, of the ladder of secret contemplation, I must observe that the chief reason why it is called a ladder is, that contemplation is the science of love, which is an infused loving knowledge of God, and which enlightens the soul and at the same time kindles within it the fire of love till it shall ascend upwards step by step unto God its Creator; for it is love only that unites the soul and God." (*Dark Night* 2.18.5)

"The soul that loves God lives more in the next life than in this, because it lives rather where it loves than where it dwells, and therefore esteeming but lightly its present bodily life, cries out: 'Let the vision and Your beauty kill me.'" (*Spiritual Canticle* 11.16)

"The soul, then, should keep in mind that it is now making greater progress than it could make by any efforts of its own, though it be wholly unconscious of that progress. God Himself is carrying it in His own arms, and thus it happens that it is not aware that it is advancing. Though it thinks that it is doing nothing, yet in truth more is done than if itself were the agent; for God Himself is working." (*Living Flame* 3.67)

"O souls, now that God shows you mercies so great, leading you into solitude and recollection, withdrawing you from the labours of sense, do not return thereto. " (Living Flame 3.75)

"The first effect [within the soul through its union with Himself] is the awakening of God in the soul, and that in gentleness and love. The second is the breathing of God in the soul, and that in grace and bliss given in that breathing. The effect of this upon the soul is to make it love Him sweetly and tenderly. " (*Living Flame* 4.2)

"O how blessed is that soul which is ever conscious of God reposing and resting within it. How necessary it is for such a soul to flee from the matters of this world, to live in great tranquillity, so that nothing whatever shall disturb the Beloved 'at His repose.'" (*Living Flame* 4.16)

For more books from *My Catholic Life!* visit our websites at:

www.mycatholic.life

www.catholic-daily-reflections.com

www.divinemercy.life

Made in the USA
Columbia, SC
29 August 2020